MW00896389

John Sadowsky

THE NEW MARKETING:
Social media, email, and the art of storytelling

Acknowledgments

For me, writing a book is a journey along a road that often turns out longer and more tortuous than anticipated. Along the way this time, many individuals assisted me in small but important ways. Rather than attempt to list them all here, and risk leaving someone out, I have made a conscious effort to thank each one personally.

To the relatively small group who made more significant contributions, I am deeply grateful, for I could not have made the journey without their efforts and support.

Nick Heys provided the idea and the inspiration for this book. He and the team at Emailvision facilitated the research, introduced me to clients, assisted with interviews, and taught me a great deal about the ins and outs of email and social media marketing. Without their help and guidance, the book would never have materialized.

Grenoble Ecole de Management underwrote some of the research and lent logistical support. Personally, I am particularly thankful to dean Thierry Grange and to associate dean Loïck Roche, both of whom have encouraged my research and writing for the past fifteen years.

Esther Vogelpoel helped edit several of the chapters. Her husband Michael was able to recover several lost files that had mysteriously vanished after a late-night computer crash.

Ethel Sadowsky proofread the entire manuscript and reminded me of most of the rules of grammar and syntax that I have a tendency to forget.

My manager, assistant, and friend Claire Legrand organized the logistics, designed much of the layout and gave some timely advice about content. She also read the final proofs of the manuscript over and over, managing to retain her sense of humor in the moments when I had lost mine.

My partner, Birgit Romme, was "chief sounding board" for content and style. She also helped do the research and provided much needed moral support throughout the entire journey.

"This book is a practical guide to using social-media tools to express a brand's true nature. It is powerful, clear, and insightful."

— GUY KAWASAKI, Author of *Enchantment: The Art of Changing Hearts, Minds, and Actions*

"For the past several years, John Sadowsky has been a driving force in our activities at the Swiss Consulate, helping Swiss entrepreneurs learn to tell their stories of identity. Personally, I have benefited greatly from John's teaching. He has helped me to better understand how to communicate the essence of the "swissnex" brand, and our diverse set of activities, to our stakeholders. In his latest book, John shows how the art of storytelling applies to modern marketing and branding. It is a masterful, big picture look at modern branding, full of insight, practical advice, and fascinating stories."

— PASCAL MARMIER, Swiss Consul in Boston

"This book will change the way you approach email and social media marketing. John Sadowsky shows you how to gather your customers around your virtual campfire and share stories about your products and brand."

— NICK HEYS, Founder and CEO, Emailvision

"John Sadowksy has written a fascinating study of modern marketing, a practical guide for telling a brand story, tying together the timeless lessons of marketing and the emerging technologies of e-commerce. John Sadowsky's examples and stories give valuable lessons and insight for building a brand in today's Internet age."

— LOÏC LE MEUR, Founder and CEO of Seesmic and LeWeb Conference

"Once upon a time I thought you could influence people by presenting abstract notions and models of how the world works. This book has stirred me up and made me reconsider my communication style by shining a light on what every human being already knows at some level, but rarely puts to use. Couch your point in a story and your ideas will have greater immediate impact. More importantly, people will remember what you said. *The New Marketing: social media, email and the art of storytelling* is a useful and timely book about modern branding, with wonderful examples and stories to show us the how it should be done."

— **Pat Brans**, author of *Master the Moment: Fifty CEOs Teach You the Secrets of Time Management*

"With true insight and remarkable examples, John Sadowsky shows us how to apply the universal principles of storytelling to the modern world of e-marketing. This is truly a groundbreaking book."

— **Thierry Grange**, Dean of Grenoble Ecole de Management; Member of AACSB International Board

Table of contents

CHAPTER 1
Introduction

HOW THIS BOOK CAME TO BE

I must begin by saying that I never intended to write a book about storytelling, branding, email marketing, and social media. In fact, the idea for this writing project came about from an interesting twist of fate.

When the book *The Seven Rules of Storytelling* (*Les sept règles du storytelling*, Editions Pearson France, with co-author Loïck Roche) was released in Paris in October 2009, it seemed like a good time to catch up with my friends and associates around Paris, to show the book and give away some signed copies. Among those I contacted at that time was Nick Heys, founder and CEO of Emailvision, a fast growing global software company specialized in email and social campaign management.

Nick and I have known each other since 1999. I served as a consultant to him in the start-up phase of his company, around the issues of how an entrepreneur learns to lead and how he begins to build a corporate culture. Since Nick understands quite well my methods of leadership coaching, and since I cite examples from my work with him at several places in the book, I was quite keen to see his reaction.

After a quick read of the *Seven Rules*, Nick turned to me with an unexpected response. "All of this applies really well to the way I see the future of email and social marketing," he said. "Why don't we develop it and share it with our clients?"

Until that moment I had never considered taking on such a project. While I have long recognized the importance of storytelling in marketing, and consulted with several companies about telling their brand stories more effectively, my recent research and writing have focused more on leadership than on marketing. It was my intent to continue on that course.

However, as our conversation continued, I was increasingly intrigued by Nick's ideas. Since we first met more than a decade ago, I have considered him a visionary in direct marketing and particularly e-marketing. As we renewed our contact, I was finding his opinions on the subject of storytelling and e-marketing fascinating.

For Nick, storytelling is simply the future of email and social media marketing. As he explained, many companies have progressed through two phases in their use of email, and they are now entering a third. The first phase was about learning. Companies needed to figure out how to start using this new marketing channel; in other words, how to build a list, design an email message, and send it out.

The second phase was about leveraging new campaign management technology for performance. Businesses became progressively more concerned with deliverability optimization, testing, targeting, and automated messages. They also learned to measure the results of their campaigns and to track customer behavior.

The third phase, according to Nick, is all about relevance. In an age when consumers are inundated with email, Twitter, Facebook and other online marketing messages, how can we craft messages that cut through the clutter, such as an email newsletter or Twitter link that the recipient will open and take the time to read? That's where storytelling comes in. The best way to write messages that engage recipients and hold their attention is to tell compelling stories. And, the more we engage our target audience, the more we build trust. This leads to long-term customer retention and profitability.

As I listened to this explanation, I was intrigued enough to want to explore the matter further. Nick and I had several more conversations, over coffee or lunch, where we spoke of the growing worldwide fascination with social media, the future of email, and our shared belief in the power of storytelling. My desire to study the links between storytelling and e-marketing grew out of these meetings.

In early 2010, Nick asked if I would speak publicly with him at industry conferences and seminars, to tell of my work with storytelling as it relates to brands, and how we could learn to tell better stories with email and social media. By the time of his offer to work together again, I had gained enough knowledge and curiosity to be a willing participant, and I readily accepted. Then, in the process of preparing and presenting the initial conferences, I made several discoveries that would lead me to write this book.

My first discovery was simply that the subject – email, social media marketing, and the art of storytelling – is indeed fascinating. I learned a great deal from speaking at the various venues, from the reading, research and interviews I did to prepare, and from interacting with the audiences. Often, I listened as participants talked about their e-marketing strategies, their successes and failures, and their plans for the coming months and years. These interactions convinced me that forward-thinking companies will create the future of e-marketing, with innovative combinations of email, social media and storytelling.

As I found myself further taken by the topic, and as I began speaking in a variety of settings, my second discovery was that the role of storytelling in email and social media is truly a pertinent theme for today's audiences. Time after time, event organizers commented that "storytelling" was an unusual topic, and that it was difficult to predict levels of interest or attendance. And time after time, the turnout was far larger than anyone had anticipated. Today, my sense is that many professionals feel that the telling of authentic and poignant brand stories is a missing element in their communication, and they are ready to listen and learn about it.

While I am encouraged that the marketplace seems increasingly ready to embrace the notion of storytelling, my third discovery was that there is a true need for this book. At my conferences, the most frequent comment from individuals and companies is that they find "all this stuff" to be of great interest and at the same time difficult. In particular, they can see the value of integrating storytelling into their email and social media marketing activities, but they are struggling to do it, and looking for help. My hope is that this book will provide them some insight.

WHAT THIS BOOK IS…AND WHAT IT IS NOT INTENDED TO BE

The New Marketing: social media, email and the art of storytelling is not meant to be a description of the "state of the art", for this would be impossible. I am quite cognizant of the fact that even before its date of publication, this book will already be outdated, since the world of social media and email marketing is moving quickly and transforming itself every day. To give a small example, as I am writing this chapter in late November 2010, LinkedIn has recently announced their new Company Pages program, and the press and bloggers are already predicting a significant impact on social media marketing.

Nor is this book intended to be a portrayal of best practices. My purpose is not to write about the extraordinary accomplishments of star companies, but rather to show some of the everyday practices of companies that we can all relate to. It is my hope that this book will stimulate thought and discussion about how any organization can strengthen its brand and build its community through intelligent use of email, social media and storytelling.

In fact, as this project progressed, one of the essential objectives that emerged was to write a straightforward book accessible to everyone, to tell stories in which readers could "see" themselves and their organizations.

I would like people to read and think, "We could do things like that." To this end, I have chosen numerous illustrations from businesses whose products or services we might use in the activities of daily life.

Most of the organizations I cite as extended examples have neither enormous notoriety nor vast marketing resources. They would certainly not be considered hot, trendy or sexy. Nonetheless, quite a few of them have achieved remarkable results by combining storytelling and digital media. They serve as proof that the practices I describe for building brands and organizing brand communities can be utilized by anybody.

Chapter-by-chapter structure

Chapter 1 is this introduction.

Chapter 2, "The power of story", is a general explanation of some of the reasons why storytelling is such a powerful communication tool.

Chapter 3, "Leadership and branding: the similarities", explains how the principles I have developed in my leadership coaching also apply very well to marketing and branding.

Chapter 4, "The current state of branding: some trends", enumerates five trends that are changing the world of marketing in general, and Internet marketing in particular.

Chapter 5, "Managing the community", provides ideas about how any organization can use the powerful combination of email, social media and storytelling for interaction with its brand community.

Chapter 6, "The Case of Filofax" is an interview with Jessica Stephens, Group Marketing Manager, a conversation that touches on many of the book's major topics.

CHAPTER 2
The power
of story

MY JOURNEY TO STORY

People often ask me how I came to believe so much in the power of story and storytelling. On the one hand, the answer is straightforward. As a coach of leaders and entrepreneurs, I came to believe in it because it works. Leaders inspire and teach with their stories of identity. Brands do as well.

On the other hand, if the concept of storytelling has taken center stage in much of the work I do today, my own path to discovering it was somewhat circuitous.

As I look back, I think that even as a schoolboy I observed my teachers and coaches with a certain fascination for how leaders communicate. Why are some individuals so effective at motivating those around them with their words?

This interest in how leaders motivate continued into my adult years. When choosing a subject for my doctoral thesis in business administration, I decided to explore the question of a leader's discourse and the elements that make it effective. My research led me unequivocally to the conclusion that the most powerful and inspirational forms of communication are story-based.

Simultaneously, my early practice as a teacher and as a coach of business leaders was lending similar insights. As I began prodding others to find and tell their stories of identity, I discovered along with my clients and students the true power of personal narrative.

Today, with nearly 15 years of experience in the field and with an ever-growing interest in self-expression, I observe with increased attention and awareness what works best in the speeches or presentations of business and political figures. Time and again I am led to the same conclusion: Outstanding leaders weave their life experience into personal stories that they use to teach, motivate and influence others.

When I listen to the speeches of inspirational leaders, I see again and again the impact of storytelling on an audience. Barack Obama, for example, is a masterful storyteller who relied on his personal stories of identity virtually every day of his 2008 campaign for the American presidency.

At the same time, storytelling is not just for politicians and CEOs. It is an increasingly important skill in today's world, whenever convincing and inspiring others is the goal. I am convinced that storytelling – when it is personal and authentic – is the most effective way to present ideas in many contexts: sharing knowledge with one's employees and colleagues, presenting to venture capitalists, selling one's product or service, or making public statements.

Through my work with several business clients in recent years, I have come to the realization that one can apply similar approaches to branding and corporate communication. As we shall see in a subsequent chapter, both leaders and brands can improve the effectiveness and relevance of their messages by emphasizing their authentic stories of identity.

While conducting the research and interviews for this book, one of the trends that emerged clearly was an increased awareness of the importance of telling and sharing stories among members of a brand community. This phenomenon is certainly not surprising. Since the beginning of time, humans have loved to share their stories. Today, the Internet in general – and social media and email in particular – provide vehicles for spreading stories as never before.

This chapter explores briefly some of the conclusions of my personal experiments with story. I explain some of the reasons why storytelling is such an effective form of communication.

One word of caution: With the concepts I present in this chapter, and with the many arguments in favor of story-based discourse, I do not wish to imply that we should abandon abstract analysis and present everything in story form. Rather, storytelling and rational argument should complement each other. What I do mean to say is that story is underutilized in modern-day communication, and that we would do well to rediscover its power.

"God made man because he loves stories."

Elie Wiesel, Nobel Peace Prize Laureate

66

"There is a general story to human existence: It is the story of how we use story."

Mark Turner, *The Literary Mind*

99

STORIES ARE UNIVERSAL, UBIQUITOUS AND CENTRAL TO ALL HUMAN CULTURE

Anthropologists tell us that the narrative impulse is as old as civilization itself. The more one studies human civilization, the more one becomes convinced that stories have been around since the beginning, and that they were man's earliest form of communication, distraction and entertainment. Since cave dwellers first drew on their walls, storytelling has been there to help human beings navigate through life.

As Danish author Karen Blixen once proclaimed: "In the beginning was the story."

Stories seem to touch something primal in the human psyche. As school children, we learn that all of history's great civilizations are characterized by their tendency to create mythic stories. In fact, every culture ever studied has used story as the primary method of teaching group norms and codes of conduct.

All cultures have their traditional keepers of the values, and they are always master storytellers. The Native American shaman, the European troubadour or raconteur, the West African griot, the Hindu pundit, or the Celtic bard never speak to their partisans with logic and fact. Their most powerful communication tool is the universal language of story. The great French literary theorist Roland Barthes is both eloquent and categorical about the role of narrative in history: "The narratives of the world are without number… the narrative is present at all times, in all places, in all societies; the history of narrative begins with the history of mankind; there does not exist, and never has existed, a people without narratives."

For Ursula Le Guin, feminist spokeswoman and author of *Dancing at the Edge of the World*, the storytelling impulse is common to the entire human race, transcending differences of race, culture and religion: "In the tale, in the telling, we are all one blood."

Stories have the power to unite and inspire us because they have universal appeal. Human fascination with stories and storytelling transcends the barriers of age, culture and time.

"

"Man is at all times a teller of stories, he lives
surrounded by his stories and the stories of
others; he sees everything that happens to him
through them, and he tries to live his life as if he
were recounting it."

Jean-Paul Sartre, French philosopher (1905-1980)

"

STORIES ARE POWERFUL BECAUSE
OUR LIVES ARE STORIES

The act of storytelling is shared by all of humanity. Stories are a common bond for all human beings for a simple reason: our lives are stories. Every individual life contains characters, plots, scripts, and all the ingredients found in a good story.

If we stop for a moment to consider how our brains work, we realize that we swim in a sea of intertwined narratives. In our minds every day are the stories we tell ourselves, the ones we exchange with others, along with the ones we imagine telling or would like to tell. All of these stories are then reworked into our master narrative, the story of our own lives that we relate constantly to ourselves, in an ongoing virtual monologue.

These personal stories, the ones we tell ourselves constantly, are the way we understand and order our world. In a sense, we organize the world around us to fit into our stories.

For psychologist Gail Sheehy, this phenomenon of internal organizing and storytelling is so pervasive that we cannot shut it off. In *New Passages: Mapping Your Life across Time*, she explains how narrative-based thought dominates our minds, and how it comes to guide our lives: "Each of us tells our own personal life story to ourselves, every day. The 'mind chatter' that rushes through our brains at two hundred words per minute when we're not concentrating on something else becomes the story we are living…The mind is formed to an astonishing degree by the act of inventing and censoring ourselves. We create our own plot line. And that plot line soon turns into a self-fulfilling prophecy… The way people tell their stories becomes so habitual that they finally become recipes for structuring experience itself, for laying down routes into memory and finally for guiding their lives."

"

"Just look at what we remember from childhood. We remember the wolf who 'huffed and puffed until he blew the house down,' whereas most of us don't remember squat from math class."

Annette Simmons, *The Story Factor*

"

Stories are the way we learn and remember

If we consider our most vivid memories of childhood, very often they involve stories we were told. Our earliest experiences are entrenched in our minds with stories attached to them.

So, if we "don't remember squat from math class", what do we remember from our days in school? Artificial intelligence guru Roger Schank lends some insight when he comments: "A good teacher is not one who explains things correctly but one who couches explanations in a memorable format."

And what exactly is a memorable format? One thing I have learned from my years of teaching both undergraduate and graduate students: If you want people to learn and truly remember something, find a way to present it to them in story form. Story-based discourse is simply far more memorable and meaningful than any other form of communication.

Years after they graduate, many students come back to me with insights gleaned from the stories I told or the cases we studied in class. Rarely do they comment that they remember a brilliant lecture or a theoretical model!

My experience is not unique. Most students and teachers who reflect on how we learn will come to understand that the human memory is narrative.

As children, we remember things by turning them into stories, and this form of recall continues throughout life. Indeed, story seems to glide effortlessly into our memory, while we often struggle mightily to retain facts, rational arguments and abstract concepts.

Story is powerful because of its ability to simplify the complex, while at the same time adding an element of excitement. Stories are memorable because they are vivid, dramatic, and concrete at the same time. They leave us with colorful images and also something tangible to hold in our minds.

Since they are so easy to remember, good stories will stay in people's memories and tend to be retold again and again.

"

"Children grow into adults by learning stories."

Alisdaire MacIntyre, moral philosopher

"

STORIES ARE THE WAY WE MAKE SENSE OF THE WORLD, FROM A YOUNG AGE

Storytelling is certainly one of the first uses of language. As soon as parents sense a child's ability to comprehend, the telling of stories begins.

And thus, as it has forever been, children throughout the world first learn by hearing simple stories, classic tales of good and evil, magical adventures where the forces of light and darkness clash. It is through hearing these uncomplicated stories that children come to understand life. Every culture's time-honored fairy tales contain the same recognizable patterns, events, and characters.

In the 1970s, renowned child psychiatrist Bruno Bettelheim, who studied fairy tales in great depth, came to the conclusion that it is indeed through stories that children learn to think. The first simple stories teach the child to reflect on his problems, on how to structure his world, on how to make sense of his emotions and how to find solutions to life's early dilemmas.

As Bettelheim explains, children <u>need</u> the classic story patterns to make sense of their daily experience in the real world.

Not only do children become creators and consumers of stories, their interaction with adults turns them into story *tellers* at a young age. As parents and teachers encourage youngsters to recount what happened to them, narrative thought patterns come to dominate a child's cognition in general. Developing narrative competence is critical to the process of learning to think and to deal with complexity.

The narrative form, psychologists now believe, is absolutely central to the process of learning to think. As the eminent psychologist and writer Jerome Bruner describes: "It's the only way children have of organizing the world, of organizing experience… they turn things into stories, and when they try to make sense of their life they use the storied version of their experience as the basis for further reflection. If they don't catch something in a narrative structure, it doesn't get remembered very well, and it doesn't seem to be accessible for further mulling over."

"

"Intelligence, for machines as well as for humans, is the telling of the right story at the right time, in the right way…In the future, machines that we interact with will have to be good storytellers."

Roger Schank, *Tell me a story: Narrative and intelligence*

"

THE MIND IS NARRATIVE. STORIES ARE THE ESSENTIAL BUILDING BLOCKS OF ALL HUMAN THOUGHT

As we have seen, children think and organize their world in story form. Increasingly, new studies are finding that this phenomenon continues into adulthood. In spite of all efforts to turn us into logical, analytical, linear thinkers, human beings think in narrative rather than in logical forms.

Stories are so powerful and engaging because they mirror human thought. They are the building blocks of the mind.

Narrative vs. paradigmatic thinking: One of the great projects of the 18th century Enlightenment was to replace narrative knowledge with scientific (or paradigmatic) knowledge, which was said to be the only "legitimate" form of knowledge. With the emerging emphasis on science to provide rational and objective analysis of all things, narrative ways of knowing were widely discounted and distrusted. The effort to reduce all knowledge to analytic propositions reached its peak in the late 20th century.

Among psychologists, the tide may be turning. Today, a growing number of researchers are proclaiming the value of narrative knowledge, suggesting that people actually think in story form, rather than in logical or rational forms. This change in attitude is happening because studies are increasingly showing that it is by the natural process of creating stories that human beings effectively <u>learn</u> to think.

Despite all attempts since the Enlightenment to convince us otherwise, recent discoveries are demonstrating that story is the native language of the brain. In fact, we may indeed be "hardwired" to think in story form.

**"The everyday mind is essentially literary...
the mental instrument I call narrative or story is
basic to human thinking."**

Mark Turner, *The Literary Mind*

"Humans are not really set up
to understand logic."

Roger Schank, *Tell me a story: Narrative and intelligence*

Psychologists are increasingly finding that we may be "hardwired" to think in story form.

Two examples of eminent thinkers who are convinced that all human thought is based on story:

Roger Schank: In *Tell me a story: Narrative and intelligence*, Schank, a leading visionary in artificial intelligence, explains his belief that the computer's inability to understand narrative is holding back progress in this field. True artificial intelligence, he explains, will be possible only when machines can tell and understand stories, since this is the way humans think. For Schank, "storytelling and understanding are functionally the same thing…In the end all we have, machine or human, are stories and methods of finding and using those stories." A truly intelligent machine may not be possible today, since such a machine would need to mimic human interaction. In other words, it would be capable of understanding stories and responding with appropriate stories from its memory.

Mark Turner: A professor of cognitive science at Case Western Reserve University and author of *The Literary Mind*, Turner did more than simply speculate or theorize that stories teach us to think. He worked extensively with neuroscientists to understand the inner workings of the brain. In his research, Turner gathered impressive evidence that shows that the native language of the brain is narrative rather than scientific or logical. According to Turner, it is by creating stories that human beings discover how to reflect, to organize and make sense of the world.

While others see stories as an important element of human thought, Turner's conclusion is that stories simply

<u>are</u> human thought. As he states: "Narrative imaging – story – is the fundamental instrument of thought…It is a literary capacity indispensable to human cognition generally."

Crafting and telling stories is the natural language of the brain. We do it all the time in our minds.

"Our very identity is a collection of stories we have come to believe about ourselves."

Orson Scott Card, *Maps in a mirror*

"When we know our stories, we know ourselves."

Noel Tichy, *The Leadership engine*

"We are our stories...That has always been true."

Daniel Pink, *A whole new mind why right brainers will rule the future*

STORIES DEFINE WHO WE ARE, PROVIDE OUR SENSE OF SELF, AND OUR SENSE OF MEANING

A human being's sense of self is determined by the stories he comes to tell and believe about himself. We define ourselves by the stories we tell, to ourselves and to others.

What do we do when we want someone to know us? We give them our life stories, we share stories of our childhoods, our school years, our first loves, our most important experiences, how we developed our points of view, and so on. Our stories allow others to get inside our minds and our lives.

Our personal narratives define our own image of who we are. They allow us to create meaning in our lives.

The act of *telling* our stories is fundamental to the human search for meaning. We use stories to reinvent ourselves, to remain vibrant. As renowned philosopher Sam Keen explains: "When we tell our stories to one another, we, at one and the same time, find the meaning of our lives and are healed from our isolation and loneliness…We don't know who we are until we hear ourselves speaking the drama of our lives to someone we trust to listen with an open mind and heart."

When we tell our personal stories of identity, we reprocess and reconnect the experiences of our lives to find our sense of meaning. Without these stories of identity, our lives cannot be meaningful.

Without stories of identity, we lose our sense of self and our sense of meaning. As Canadian journalist and author Robert Fulford tells us: "To discover we have no story is to acknowledge that our existence is meaningless."

Losing our stories can have dire consequences. Celebrated psychiatrist and author Keith Ablow explains suicide in terms of a disconnect from one's stories of identity: "I think the thing that binds together most people who go on to take their lives is that they have an inability to imagine the next chapter in their life stories."

"

"As our primitive ancestors sat around the fire carving spearheads and eating blackberries they told stories which in time were woven into a tapestry of myth and legend. These tales were the first encyclopedia of human knowledge. They explained where the world came from, why there were people, why snakes have no legs, why corn smut stops birth hemorrhages, why conch shells are sacred, why coyotes howl at night, and why the gods put fire and death on earth…Stories told the people of a tribe who they were, where they had been, where they were going, and how to stay friendly with the spirits."

Sam Keen, author and philosopher

"

STORIES DEFINE OUR COMMUNITIES, PROVIDE A SENSE OF COLLECTIVE IDENTITY, A SENSE OF BELONGING

Anthropologists have long recognized that stories create the sense of cultural identity, the tribal element that defines and binds communities. In olden times, communal sharing of stories happened quite naturally; as tribes gathered for reasons of necessity and survival, their stories became the vehicle for defining and sustaining the norms and traditions of the group.

In modern times as well, the tribal narrative remains the way a group defines its identity, its shared values, its sense of self, and its concept of who belongs and who does not. Many of today's organizations are discovering the power of stories to provide work groups with a sense of shared identity.

Stories are the most powerful vehicles for transmitting a group's norms and guiding members' behavior. By showing examples, stories give a concrete context to abstract values.

Today, as in ancient times, any group's culture is passed down through the stories its members tell and retell. Stories of identity are extremely influential, because they tend to be told over and over again and thus come to determine behavior, without dictating it. Storytelling allows us to instill group values in a way that keeps people thinking for themselves.

In the world of modern technology, communities continue to come together and define themselves around the stories they share. What is a Facebook group, if not a virtual community that shares its stories and finds those stories meaningful?

We should study these groups in anthropological terms, pay attention to their stories, listen to them, and understand them. Knowing an organization, and truly comprehending it in all its complexity, means having a thorough understanding of its stories.

"Stories are the single most powerful form of human communication. This has been true all over the world for thousands of years and is still just as true today in our organizations, communities, and families. If you want someone to remember information and believe it, your best strategy in almost every case is to give them the information in the form of a story."

Peg Neuhauser, *Corporate Legends and Lore*

STORIES ARE OUR MOST EFFECTIVE FORM OF COMMUNICATION

Stories <u>engage us on multiple levels</u>. Some researchers claim that stories are powerful communicators because they touch the entire brain—the left (logical and rational) hemisphere as well as the right (feeling) hemisphere, the subconscious as well as the conscious. Thus, we simultaneously *feel* and *understand* stories.

While I am not qualified to speak of the hemispheres of the brain, experience has taught me that storytelling reaches us in holistic ways and on multiple levels. Stories touch both our emotional and our rational sides. They allow the listener to *see and feel* information, rather than merely understand it.

Stories <u>enter the mind naturally</u>. Since the human mind is narrative, we are naturally predisposed to create, remember and tell stories. The process of following a story is easy, enjoyable and almost automatic. By contrast, logical explanations force us into an abstract way of thinking, which our minds tend to find tiring.

Stories are easily remembered and retold, since they provide context and flow. Fact and logic, on the other hand, do not provide this context or flow. While it is difficult to remember the facts and technical detail of a complex presentation, we can often remember and reproduce even the most complex and convoluted of stories.

Because stories enter our minds naturally and without resistance, we embrace them more easily than any other form of discourse. When speakers try to convince us with concepts and theory, we often look for flaws in their reasoning. When a speaker tells a personal story, we tend to relax, let it in and accept it.

"The abstract way of thinking leaves us as perpetual spectators, self-conscious and external – turning us into voyeurs who observe the world…By contrast, the narrative way of thinking is internal and immersive and self-forgetting and attached to the full richness of tacit understanding. Through a story, life invites us to come inside as a participant."

Stephen Denning, *The Springboard*

Story provides a vicarious experience and invites us to participate: When a speaker tells a story to an audience, she seeks to build a bridge between parallel lives – hers and the listeners'. If it is well told, we feel a story deeply because it touches something in our common experience, our common humanity. We can empathize with the teller, and thus a vicarious "experience" is generated.

When we present a business idea, we would like the listeners to *feel* it vicariously, and with all the passion we feel. If we paint vivid pictures with our stories, it is one way to truly stand out amid the seemingly never-ending stream of slideshows and company-speak of modern corporate life.

Stories create energy and excitement: Stories engage an audience simply because they are more enjoyable than other forms of oral expression. Stories enhance attention, make connections with the listeners, and create anticipation. With a story, we can add feeling, vitality, drama and vivid imagery to any speech or presentation.

A good story generates energy, so the teller is more persuasive. We have all felt the difference between a speaker who expounds on his beliefs with rational argument, and one who tells the stories that bring his beliefs to life.

We embrace stories because they are <u>non-invasive</u>. They don't preach or force their ideas on us. We don't resist them because they don't tell us what to think or do. They allow us to think for ourselves, to participate, to draw our own conclusions. Stories stimulate, rather than direct or channel, the mind of the listener.

Story lets us instill values in a way that allows people to keep thinking for themselves. When a speaker states, "We always put the customer first", listeners tend to be doubtful or even cynical about this common message. In contrast, when we hear the stories of employees who have provided outstanding customer service, the concept becomes immediately more credible.

66

"It has always been the prime function of mythology and rite to supply the symbols that carry the human spirit forward, in counteraction to those other constant human fantasies that tend to tie it back."

Joseph Campbell, mythologist and author

99

STORIES PROVIDE A SENSE OF PURPOSE AND POSSIBILITY

The eminent mythologist Joseph Campbell called mythology "the song of the universe", a philosophical roadmap for the human condition, a guide to help us through any experience or trial we might encounter. He believed that the classic tales of humanity could be an inspiration to us in our daily lives. With a mythical perspective, all experience becomes empowering; without it, life can appear as nothing more than a meaningless series of ups and downs.

Since the beginning of time, story, myth and legend have inspired humans to greater heights. Stories give our lives meaning by showing us a world of purpose and possibility. The ability to see our own existence as a coherent story, rather than a sequence of unrelated events, increases the possibility of focused and purposeful action.

Emblematic stories, legends and myths are common to all the world's cultures because every society has used them as a source of inspiration. Historians, anthropologists and folklorists tell us that stories are not only common to all the world's cultures, but also that the fundamental stories of mankind follow the same universal, archetypal patterns.

We are on familiar terms with these stories, we recognize their characters and their symbols, because their classic patterns have been reproduced and retold over and over throughout the ages. We see potential roles for ourselves in these stories, since they are the stories we remember from childhood, from the literature we read, and from the films we watch.

"Isn't it queer: there are only two or three human stories, and they go on repeating themselves as fiercely as if they had never happened before."

Willa Cather, *O pioneers!*

"

"If we ignore the technology for a moment and consider the stories and themes, mass culture appears to circle endlessly around the same trail, meeting on its path again and again the same characters in roughly the same stories. It is a good general rule that the more successful a work of mass culture, the more it will conform to a pattern with which our grandparents were on intimate terms."

Robert Fulford, *The triumph of narrative:storytelling in the age of mass culture*

"

When considering the history of narrative, it is indeed striking that there are only a few human stories, and that they have repeated themselves, over and over, throughout the ages. In fact, there is a single storyline or pattern that has dominated mass culture, from ancient theatre to modern-day movies such as *Star Wars* or *The Lord of the Rings*: the Hero's Journey.

The hero archetype is ever-present in the world's stories for a simple reason: More than any other type of narrative, the heroic tale gives us a sense of meaning and possibility, a feeling that something larger exists, something we could reach for in our own lives, in our businesses, and in our careers. Participating in a heroic journey gives us a sense of destiny.

Mythical heroes are sources of inspiration, since these heroes depict the timeless struggle of the human spirit to triumph over adversity. Stories of larger-than-life heroes expand our notion of what we might accomplish in our lives. Above all, we identify with the Hero's Journey because we long for adventure. We dream of worlds of infinite possibility, where we might define and strive for noteworthy goals.

Since his beginnings, man has loved to share heroic tales. In today's age of mass communication, we remain fascinated by the heroic stories of others, and we long to become stars in our own hero stories. With the advent of social media, ordinary people can become heroes and share their heroic stories with the world. For example, Matt (*http://www.wherethehellismatt.com*) became a hero for many, and created a remarkable Internet movement, simply by dancing and inviting others around the world to dance with him.

Since the Hero's Journey is so powerful, ubiquitous and influential, I will lay out its basic pattern in the pages that follow, show an example from popular culture, and discuss the relevance of heroic tales in the world of business and marketing.

"The Hero ventures forth from the world of the common day into a region of supernatural wonder: fabulous forces are there encountered and a decisive victory is won: the hero comes back from this mysterious adventure with the power to bestow boons on his fellow man."

Joseph Campbell, *The Hero with a Thousand Faces*

The Hero's Journey follows a pattern that is elegant and simple, through four phases: separation, descent, initiation, and return. In the separation phase, the hero is pulled from his ordinary world by a call to adventure. Often, the hero is comfortable in the "ordinary world", but at the same time uneasy, as if he doesn't completely "fit" there somehow. His world is familiar and easy, but something is missing in the hero's life, whether or not he can define it.

When the call to adventure comes, there are moments of hesitation. Often, the hero ignores or even refuses the call. In the end, though, frequently at the urging of a wise elder, the hero does decide to answer the call, and the journey away from the familiar begins.

In the second phase, the hero plunges into the underworld, the darkness, the netherworld, or the "belly of the whale". As with this entire journey, the concept of descent should not be taken literally. The hero's most important journey is often symbolic, with the belly of the whale representing an internal or psychic struggle. However, in some form, the hero leaves his ordinary world behind and "descends" into a special world that is unfamiliar and challenging. In this special world, the hero faces a series of trials, discovering friends and enemies along the route. He is often aided by courageous allies, by an astute mentor, and even by unknown or supernatural forces.

At some point, the hero passes through the third phase, which is some type of initiation that will transform him in a profound and lasting manner. He will enter the "innermost cave" and encounter his supreme ordeal. Either in a real and physical way, or in a symbolic sense, the hero "seizes the sword", summoning all his courage and inner strength to win the ultimate victory.

The fourth phase is the return to the ordinary world, a journey home which may be fraught with its own perils and adventures. In the end, the hero does return, completing the mythical cycle, but he returns transformed, often with new wisdom, or with an "elixir" that changes his life and the lives of those around him.

In many cases, the end of the story mirrors the beginning, except that the adventure, the journey to the special world, has changed the hero forever. While the hero may return to a situation that resembles his former life in the ordinary world, his existence now has new meaning. The wisdom, the understanding and the skills acquired on the journey allow him to perform acts of skill and bravery that would have frightened him in times past. Upon return the hero and his followers are able to do things they could never have imagined before their adventure. As Campbell says, the hero has now become master of two worlds.

The Hero's Journey is part of our daily lives, more than we realize. For proof, we need look no further than popular novels and movies such as *Star Wars* or *The Lord of the Rings*.

A rapid examination of *The Lord of the Rings* trilogy (Tolkien's novels or Peter Jackson's films) reveals a story that follows the classic Hero structure and portrays archetypal characters. At the outset, Frodo Baggins lives in the ordinary world of the Shire. When a ring given to him by his uncle Bilbo turns out to be the One Ring of Power, the wizard Gandalf urges Frodo to take the ring from the Shire in order to prevent the allies of the evil lord Sauron from finding it (call to adventure, separation).

Frodo tries to refuse the call, claiming that he does not want an adventure, and is subsequently convinced by the wise mentor Gandalf that his mission must be done. Frodo finds allies (his hobbit friends and Strider) and enemies (the Nazgul, the Orcs, and the allies of Sauroman) on his road to Rivendell, where he again is called to adventure.

For Frodo, the belly of the whale, his descent into the netherworld, is the journey to Mordor. Along the way, he again faces numerous challenges and tests, finds allies, and confronts enemies. He faces the ultimate ordeal, the innermost cave, at Mount Doom (his initiation), destroys the ring (the equivalent of seizing the sword), and then returns to the Shire, transformed by his experience. His life, and those of his fellow journeymen, is transformed forever, as he has become the master of both the ordinary world and the special world of adventure.

"Fundamentally, every business is a stage for the enactment of human myths...
Look under the surface of any organization and you will find the classical story structure that has been the foundation of most yarns and tales of adventure since the beginning of human communication."

Richard Stone, *The healing art of storytelling:a sacred journey of personal discovery*

What does all this talk of patterns, archetypes, journeys and heroes have to do with business, marketing, or modern organizations in general? Quite a lot, in fact, for why would we expect business to be any different than the rest of life? Classic business stories repeat the themes we see over and over in any culture's archetypal legends and mythology—tales of perseverance, of cunning, of rivalry and succession, of fantastic successes or tragic failures, of a hero's rise and fall or even descent into madness, of the overcoming of great odds, or of upholding one's principles despite the cost.

Researchers who have studied the corporate lore of companies such as McDonald's, Hewlett-Packard and General Electric have concluded that these corporate stories follow classic patterns of myth, legend and fairy tales, and that the Hero's Journey is alive and well in the world of business.

The Hero's Journey also has a definite place in the world of marketing and branding. For example, we have all experienced great salespeople who know how to tell stories in which the product becomes the hero. In my own quest for understanding marketing, I have often noted that winning brands exploit archetypal forms and touch their audiences in deep ways. The most successful ones – brands such as Coca-Cola and Nike – make people feel like heroes, part of the group of consumers who have made the winning choice.

Later in this book, when we examine some of the best practices in managing a community, we will see that hero stories can bind brand communities together. As consumers, we join brand communities, become their "fans", for the way they make us feel. If the brand makes us feel a part of something different and special, it can take us on a heroic journey.

One of the objectives of an enterprise should be to make its key constituents, particularly its employees and customers, feel and behave like heroes. In chapter 5, "Managing the Community", I will present numerous ideas that can help accomplish this goal.

"

"After all we've been sitting around campfires for 100,000 years listening to each other's stories – our brains are organized by narrative... The media is the current campfire."

Gloria Steinem, author, activist, feminist legend

"

STORIES ARE POWERFUL BECAUSE THEY LEND THEMSELVES TO VIRAL TRANSMISSION

The quote from Gloria Steinem on the preceding page sums things up well. Story has always been the way we share our lives and experiences. Today, our stories are the messages, the photos and the videos we post, and the most popular ones can spread almost instantaneously across the Web.

Indeed, we live in a viral culture. This culture can label an idea or a story culturally significant in a flash. It rewards bravado and confers attention for fleeting moments. Today, it seems that everybody wants to be somebody, and that means having a good personal story to tell. Such stories spread in this culture because we have become savvy marketers of ourselves, and we view with admiration the self-promoting initiatives of others.

Viral marketing has come a long way. Before the Internet era, companies would make commercials and hope that consumers would find them "cool" enough to talk about with their friends. As we will see in chapter 4, companies today try to create viral effects by planting videos on their websites or on social sites. Better yet, they are making videos and encouraging their communities of friends and fans to take them viral. And better still, they are prodding users to produce the videos that the wider community of users then takes viral.

Before the Internet era, it took months or years to create an extensive viral buzz throughout the world. In our time, simple videos such as the one where "scientists" mix Diet Coke and Menthos to create explosions can get over one million views in less than a month. That story went around the globe simply by virtue of friends telling friends.

In mid-July 2010, Old Spice and actor Isaiah Mustafa collaborated to seed various social networks with invitations to ask questions of Mustafa's character, a handsome shirtless man of supreme confidence and humor. The ensuing Internet buzz was nothing short of spectacular.

Throughout the day, responses were tracked. Users who contributed interesting questions or were high-profile people on social networks received direct and personalized responses, nearly in real-time, in the form of quick and humorous YouTube videos.

Even to individuals who did not receive the direct responses, the stories created in this initiative felt so rapid and custom-made that many watched for hours, fascinated by this Internet "happening". They were transfixed by the episodic event, as it evolved into an ongoing saga produced right before their eyes.

Numerous blogs began commenting that the Old Spice endeavor was dominating online and water-cooler conversations everywhere, causing the buzz to escalate further. On the following day, influential bloggers were somewhat in awe, calling the effort spectacular, even stating that anyone connected to the Internet could not help but notice. One of them proclaimed that if you didn't have your computer on yesterday, "or if you live in a cave, you need to be aware of the fact that Old Spice owned the Internet yesterday."

The extraordinarily simple and elegant genius of the Old Spice incident is how they engaged viewers to tell and spread the stories, creating the viral effect. In fact, they are merely using the age-old power of story *telling*, in combination with the modern-day power of the Internet for story *sharing*. There is no better way to encourage the spreading of a message than to allow users to watch themselves, or people like them, become heroes in their story.

SUMMARY OF CHAPTER 2

Since we have covered a lot of ground in this chapter, it is perhaps useful to review some of the subchapter headings, as they remind us of the reasons why storytelling is the most powerful and effective form of discourse known to man.

Stories are powerful because our lives <u>are</u> stories.

Stories are universal, ubiquitous and central to all human culture.

Stories are the way human beings learn and remember.

Stories are the way we make sense of the world, from a young age.

Since the mind is narrative, stories are the essential building blocks of all human thought.

Stories define who we are, providing our sense of self and our sense of meaning.

Stories define our communities, providing us a sense of collective identity and a sense of belonging.

Stories offer us a sense of purpose and possibility.

Stories lend themselves to viral transmission.

CHAPTER 3
Leadership and branding: the similarities

I see a brand's self-expression as quite similar to a leader's self-expression. At the core, both are about learning to tell one's stories effectively.

INTRODUCTION TO CHAPTER 3

As I recount in chapter 1, it was Nick Heys of Emailvision who got me thinking deeply about the role storytelling will play in the future of Internet marketing. When I began speaking at e-marketing events, and preparing presentations about using storytelling in email and social media, I was reminded once again of the similarities between the coaching I do with leaders and the work of building a brand.

Indeed, leadership and branding are comparable in numerous ways. Successful leaders and successful brands connect with their audiences and build their communities. They create movements, inspire followers, and provide visions of the future. To be effective communicators, leaders and brands must learn to express themselves in ways that are by and large alike. In essence, they tell stories of who they are and why we should follow.

The ideas that I will discuss briefly in this chapter form some of the core elements of my leadership coaching: self-knowledge, authenticity, telling personal stories of identity, finding a straightforward and natural voice. With some minor adaptations, one can easily apply each of these notions to building a brand, or to "coaching" that brand in self-expression.

Throughout this chapter, these core concepts will come back again and again in various forms. They are the keys to becoming a leader, and to building a brand.

When I coach a leader, I usually begin with the concept of **self-knowledge**. Winning leaders are characterized by an enormous clarity about who they are, what truly matters to them, and where they are going. For any institution or any brand, that same clarity should exist. Brands, as well as leaders, must have unambiguous ideas about who they are and what they stand for before they can convey their messages to the world.

When we understand clearly who we are and what we stand for, we can engage others with **our stories of identity**. Both brands and leaders express themselves through their stories of who I am, where I come from (for a brand, these are often origin or founder stories), and why I do things the way I do. The most effective of these stories are **simple**, **personal**, and **authentic**.

The remainder of this chapter focuses on some of the salient concepts I have outlined here, and a few others that are central to my leadership coaching. Since storytelling takes center stage in my work with leaders, and since brands can learn to use story in similar ways, the concepts of this chapter lay a foundation for the rest of the book. Understanding how brands communicate effectively by telling their stories will help us appreciate the vital role that storytelling can play in email and social media marketing.

The heart of leadership has little to do with style or charisma. It is more about finding your true nature and your natural voice.
In the same vein, the essence of branding is not about creating hype and buzz. Brands, also, need to focus on finding and expressing their unique nature.

CHARISMA, STYLE, HYPE AND BUZZ

Ever since I began coaching leaders some fifteen years ago, I have been confronted time and again with a widespread misconception that society harbors about leadership. Many individuals enter the coaching relationship with the request that we work on their "charisma". They think that the key to becoming a more effective leader is to appear to be more charismatic.

And often, the first thing I have to tell them is to forget about charisma, for it is irrelevant to one's leadership development. Of all the effective leaders I have worked with or observed, only a small number have what I would call a charismatic personality. In addition, I am not at all sure that the charismatic ones are the most credible or authentic.

Charisma does not bring about leadership. I have come to believe that there is a basic problem with the dominant view of charisma in our society: We tend to think that leadership success is the <u>result</u> of a charismatic personality. My experience has shown that it usually happens the other way around.

Outstanding leadership does not come from charisma. It comes from finding one's true nature, one's passion, and one's natural voice. It is the authenticity of the voice and the passion that can make someone appear charismatic. Charisma is the result of leadership passion, not the cause.

I also see a problem with the concept of trying to "appear more charismatic". This problem has to do with the way we have come to see the notion of learning to lead. In our society today, we tend to look for models to follow and styles to emulate. We seek to copy the oratory techniques of inspirational speakers, or the behaviors of "winning" leaders. In other words, we search outside ourselves for guidelines and blueprints, when the path to becoming a leader is inside of us.

When I work with someone on self-expression, I emphasize that it has to happen from the inside out. First, understand who you are at the core, then learn to express who you are in your natural voice. That voice may become charismatic, or it may not. A natural and authentic voice is more important than a charismatic one.

Hype does not make a brand. Like leaders, brands are made from the inside out. For a brand, the central issues are the same as for a leader. In the current age of Internet marketing, people often ask me how to create "buzz" using social media and email. When I hear such questions, I think it is somehow quite similar to the leader who wants to be a better speaker or appear more charismatic.

Please don't get me wrong. I am not saying that brands should not want to create a buzz, or that leaders should not care about the techniques for delivering their messages. Rather, I would say that charisma or buzz should not be the goal, and that we should not make

the common mistake of focusing too heavily on issues
of style and appearance.

Branding, like leadership, is a journey for the long term.
Rather than look for a quick road to fame through hype
or buzz, focus on understanding and refining your core
messages. Above all, a brand builds itself by knowing its
true nature and learning to express itself authentically.

"A great brand knows itself."

Scott Bedbury, *New Brand World: Eight Principles for Achieving Brand Leadership in the 21st Century*

SELF-KNOWLEDGE

Scott Bedbury should know something about branding. He is the author of *New Brand World: Eight Principles for Achieving Brand Leadership in the 21st Century*. In the mid-1990s, he was a driving force in turning Starbucks into a global brand. Previous to that, he had directed Nike's worldwide advertising efforts and was responsible for initiating the "Just Do It" branding campaign.

When I first saw Bedbury's quote about a great brand knowing itself, it was a vivid reminder of how much leadership development and brand building use similar concepts, at least in my view. In fact, I often tell my clients and seminar participants that leadership begins with the simple advice of the Oracle of Delphi of ancient Greece: "know thyself".

Knowing one's true nature is the key to leadership and to branding, and the road to one's true nature begins with self-exploration. When I coach a leader or advise a company about its brand, I invariably start the process with an exercise I call the "inner journey to self-knowledge."

When we do this "inner journey", we explore our entire existence, from our earliest memories to the present. We look to gain a clear understanding of who we are, what we stand for, what truly matters in our lives, what our core beliefs are, and how we see our future.

A leader must make the journey inward – to self-discovery and self-knowledge – before making the journey outward, to influencing and inspiring others. It is our life stories, our examination and understanding of our life experience, that allow us to be coherent and compelling in expressing ourselves to our listeners.

Outstanding brands, like outstanding leaders, know and use their life stories. Thus, for a brand we do the same journey inward, to remind ourselves of the stories of the founders, the history, the core values, the "who we are" and "what we stand for" of the company. From our inner journey come the stories that allow us to make deep connections with our customers and other stakeholders.

Since great brands know themselves, they have a clear vision of what they stand for, and where they would like to go. They have modern stories that are ever-evolving, and at the same time they are conscious of their rich traditions and core philosophies. Such brands would include Harley-Davidson, IKEA, BMW, and Levi's.

Take the example of Levi's Jeans. The company has a story that goes back to the Great California Gold Rush of the mid-19th century. They still display photos of miners from the 1850s wearing the original trousers of durable brown cloth, or images of the first denim jeans from the 1870s. At the same time, Levi's updates its image with photos and stories from its user community. For example, its Facebook page encourages "New American Pioneers" and consumers around the world to engage, meet others, and share modern tales of how they use the current products and styles.

For a great brand, the story never ends!

Two of the fundamental principles of communication, for a leader or for a brand, are <u>inspirational storytelling</u> and <u>authenticity</u>. Much of my coaching is about helping individuals and companies discover and tell their personal stories of identity. At the same time, I warn that we should never tell stories that we cannot completely embody.

Authenticity comes from truly living our stories.

STORIES OF IDENTITY

The importance of personal stories of identity: Ultimately, we lead by autobiography. That is, we express our character in the stories we tell. The more we come to know ourselves, the more we can explain our true nature by telling our personal stories of identity. These autobiographical tales – for example, stories of who I am, where I come from, and why I do what I do – form the basis for our legitimacy and credibility.

If an individual wants to lead any type of change, his stories of identity must exemplify the values and behavior he encourages others to emulate.

Former British Prime Minister Margaret Thatcher is an interesting case study in leading by autobiography. Whatever one's political views, one cannot help but admire this remarkable woman's ability to lead by using her personal stories of identity. In effect, Thatcher transformed a nation by presenting herself as a change agent whose personal values mirrored precisely the principles necessary for putting a "lost" Britain back on course. After convincing the British to vote for a change of direction in government, she emphasized the connection between her personal story and her story for a new Britain: "The passionately interesting thing to me is that the things I learned in a small town, in a very modest home, are just the things I believe have won the election." Thatcher's stories of identity formed the foundation for her transformational leadership.

Brands too can inspire their stakeholders with their stories of identity. Timberland, an outdoor boot and apparel company with sales of $1.3 billion, communicates regularly about its desire to be a leader among socially and environmentally responsible businesses in the US and worldwide. In its public statements, the company commits to setting industry standards for community action and environmental reporting.

Stories and authenticity: Authenticity comes from "walking the talk", from absolutely no gap existing between the leader's words and actions. So, we make sure we are not only living our stories, but embodying them in visible ways. If we fail to live our stories, and if others do not observe us living them, we will lose the trust of our followers. Authenticity is about finding the right story to express our values, and then showing that we can stay true to our principles.

When Margaret Thatcher told the people of Great Britain that her childhood values of self-reliance, initiative, and decency were the remedies for their ailing nation, she had to be certain to embody these values in everything she did.

Similarly, if Timberland tells a story of commitment to the environment and social responsibility, they must show the world that they are living their pledge in their daily actions. In fact, the company's corporate headquarters demonstrates their desire to live out their story. Solar panels are in prominent view, and the vegetable gardens adjacent to the car park are tended by employees using company paid "community service hours". Produce from the gardens is sold to aid state-run food banks.

In our modern age of Internet transparency, embodying a brand's stories of identity is more important than ever. As we will see in numerous examples from later chapters, people today are cynical about anything that looks fake, and someone, somewhere will be ready to blow the whistle on any brand story that proves to be unauthentic.

Both brands and leaders use stories of identity to inspire followers. But stories of identity are not enough. They must tell stories that engage their communities.

STORIES OF ENGAGEMENT

Leaders tell and live stories that other people want to be a part of.

Effective leaders engage with their stories. They give us not only a sense of belonging, but also a sense of possibility. Their stories provide the context that makes people feel part of a larger experience.

In *True to Our Roots*, a book about his experience at Fetzer Vineyards, former CEO Paul Dolan describes how he transformed the winery by creating a vivid picture of the future that could come to life for others in the organization. His tale combined a story of identity ("we are special people") with a future story, a story about "who we can become". It was all encapsulated in a simple phrase: "Fetzer people: enhancing the quality of life." In a more protracted version, Dolan explained the vision to his people: Fetzer would be an environmentally and socially conscious company that produces wines of the highest quality and value, while at the same time embracing, and taking responsibility for, its higher societal mission.

By defining a cause, not merely a business, a mission as opposed to a task, Dolan was able to convince employees that their work was truly essential to their customers' wellbeing, and even that what they did every day mattered to the world at large. They were not merely making wine; they were enhancing the quality of life.

Successful brands are like successful leaders in the way they are able to inspire. Brands, like leaders, tell stories that others want to be a part of. They engage their communities on issues that their people, the members of the brand community, care deeply about.

One brand that succeeds in engaging its user community with a larger, more meaningful story is Pampers, the global market-share leader in baby diapers. While the product itself is a common one with a routine function, the company has managed to build an active following by positioning themselves as the people who help with all aspects of caring for an infant child.

On their Pampers Village website, they have assembled the Pampers Parenting Network, a group of leading child development specialists and medical professionals, handpicked to provide parents with free expert advice. The "Ask an Expert" section puts visitors directly in touch with the experts, who offer answers to questions about a variety of parenting concerns, such as feeding and sleeping habits.

The Pampers example is an interesting one, as it demonstrates an increasingly prevalent marketing strategy of forward-thinking brands. On their websites or Facebook pages, these brands often build a sense of community not by talking about their products and services but rather about related activities. By offering value-added content about all aspects of becoming a parent, Pampers becomes a trusted companion, a partner in a broader conversation that goes far beyond the product itself.

"Out of clutter, find simplicity."

Albert Einstein, Nobel Prize winning physicist (1879-1955)

SIMPLIFY

Albert Einstein's first rule of work was: "Out of clutter, find simplicity." It is a quote that I have used countless times in my coaching of leaders. In fact, after fifteen years of working with individuals on their self-expression, I have come to believe that there is a general human tendency to make messages overly complex. When I hear people telling their stories, making their speeches or giving their formal presentations in a corporate setting, I am usually left with the impression that the whole thing is overly cluttered. We need desperately to learn to simplify!

The most successful leaders <u>are</u> able to simplify their messages. When I observe political campaigns, I watch in particular the stories that the candidates tell to groups of voters. While I recognize that politics is quite complex, and while I certainly do not consider myself an expert analyst, I am often struck by a simple truth: the candidate who is able to simplify and clarify his messages is usually the one who wins. For example, in the 2008 US presidential election, Barack Obama stayed focused on a few themes and told his personal stories of identity in direct and concise fashion. John McCain did not.

Obama simplified his stories in order to make them clear and accessible to a wider audience. The best brands do this as well.

Branding and simplicity: Think of some of the most valuable brands in the world at the peak of their success, and consider the simplicity of their stories. Nokia was about "connecting people", Apple had "computers for the rest of us", IKEA was "making people's lives easier", Nike was encouraging us to "just do it" and Coca-Cola was bringing us "the real thing".

All of these brand messages are easy to follow, pure and graceful. We follow them because they speak to us in a primal way. They make us feel clean and wholesome, as part of a winning team.

One of my favorite tales of branding simplicity is the "Intel Inside" story. Most people who use a computer have no idea how a microprocessor works, what its precise role is, or what would make one brand superior to another. Yet, in the 1990s, Intel's "Intel Inside" advertising campaign made it and its Pentium processor household names. So today, many consumers <u>do</u> know that they want a computer with an Intel inside. The company has managed to create a simple and elegant brand story around a product that nobody sees, and that only engineers and technologists truly understand.

When consumers buy a computer with an Intel processor inside, they feel part of the winning team. As we will see in chapters 4 and 5, smaller, lesser-known companies can also bring together a brand community around simple themes. For example, mydeco.com attracts followers who are united by their "passion for design", and the French kitchenware company Mathon invites any "fan of cooking" to join them. The simplicity of their branding messages helps them attract a large follower base.

"The great question of leadership, about taking real steps on the pilgrim's path, is the great question of any individual life: how to make everything more personal."

David Whyte, *Crossing the Unknown Sea: Work as a Pilgrimage of Identity*

PERSONALIZE

David Whyte's observation about leadership echoes one of my most frequent pieces of advice to clients about improving their communication: Make it more personal.

Excellent leaders understand that the most meaningful communication happens when we reveal ourselves in personal ways. We show our passion and enthusiasm through the personal stories we tell; it is through these personal stories that we make deep, emotional connections with our audience.

My coaching experience has persuaded me unequivocally that personalization works. The most effective leaders I have worked with are not only in touch with their stories, they do not hesitate to speak from the heart about the lessons of their life experience.

The celebrated basketball coach Phil Jackson has always brought his personal stories to work with him. When Jackson took over as coach of Michael Jordan and the Chicago Bulls in 1988, he inherited a team with some of the league's most talented and spectacular players, but one which had never won a championship. From the outset, one of Jackson's central goals was to get the team's star players to join in a collective quest, to adopt a selfless attitude, and to accept that team success was more important than their individual accomplishments.

At team gatherings, Jackson began telling stories of his own life lessons, tales of his practice of Zen meditation, or of the notions of selflessness he gleaned from spending time with the Lakota Sioux tribe. As players started listening to their new coach and embracing his novel approach, a new unselfish team philosophy developed, and the NBA championship titles soon followed. In the book *Sacred Hoops*, where he recounts these events, Jackson cites the personal stories he shared with his team as one of the critical elements that led to the transformation of the Bulls' team culture and overall approach to the game.

The personalizing of brand stories: While we understand how personal stories and passion can enhance the effectiveness of a leader's discourse, how can we apply this concept to a brand?

In the age of e-marketing, the world is becoming more personal every day. Brands have opportunities to communicate with us on multiple touch points, and to use these various points to spread personal stories. For example, a company might collect user stories via email or Facebook and then circulate the most interesting ones in their newsletter. As consumers, we long for personalization. We prefer to hear the personal stories of people like us, fellow users of a product or members of the community, rather than direct corporate advertising.

Smart marketers are finding innovative ways to get users to contribute their personal tales for the benefit of the community. Bike Friday, a US-based maker of folding bicycles, asks users to send in stories and photos that answer the question "What do <u>you</u> do on a Friday?" Today, they have an impressive collection of user-generated stories, photos and videos. These personal testimonials cost the business almost nothing to generate, and they are surely the company's most credible advertising vehicle.

**"Great people make us feel
we can become great."**

Mark Twain, American author and humorist (1835-1910)

PROJECTION

When I think of this quote from Mark Twain about great people, it causes me to reflect on a notion I have come to call "projection". In part, great leaders make us feel we can become great because they allow us to dream of a future with more challenge and meaning. They "project" us into a larger story, onto a bigger stage.

The most effective leaders are continuously crafting and living larger stories, for themselves and with their followers. Such leaders often inspire with heroic stories that give others a sense of belonging to a unique and exceptional group. Often, a leader's most influential stories are the clear and simple visions of the future he offers to followers, portrayals so cogent and vivid that they transport the listener to a new reality.

We long for leadership stories that portray a meaningful future. One of the masters of this type of motivational discourse, this projection onto a larger stage, was Steve Jobs. When Jobs was their product champion in the early 1980s, the Macintosh team became a strike force to challenge the world, the ultimate heroic underdogs, taking on not only competitors but the nonbelievers inside Apple as well. They were a group of revolutionaries, insurgents, mutineers, iconoclasts. Jobs, their spiritual leader, raised the pirate flag outside the Macintosh building, and he called on Team Macintosh not only to invent the future of computing, but to put "a dent in the universe." Jobs' discourse was extremely effective, since engaging followers means not only defining a shared identity that resonates with them, but also projecting them into a future bigger and more consequential than they had previously envisioned.

As do great leaders, great brands make us feel we can become great. In fact, we look for hero stories from our brands as much as we do from our leaders. As Steve Jobs did with the Macintosh team, the best brands make participants feel like heroes.

We long for brand stories that take us beyond the mundane. The most memorable brands take us on journeys; they let us dream of putting more meaning in our lives. Patagonia incites us to enter the realm of challenge and adventure. Nike tells us to act courageously and "just do it". Starbucks invites us to explore the vast and exciting world of coffee. IKEA tells us that we can craft new things and take charge of our lives. All of these brands are projecting us into bigger life stories.

Great brands transcend the boundaries of a narrow product category and become protagonists for a larger cause. Nike, for example, extends itself far beyond building shoes and making apparel. They are advocates for the athlete, and for all of sport. As a protagonist for sports and the active lifestyle, Nike provides opinions on such issues as where sport is going, how athletes think, and how we should think and train as we try to achieve a personal best.

Brands such as Nike recognize that consumers live in an emotional world. Most people do not enjoy discussing the construction or technical merits of an athletic shoe. They get excited by last night's winning goal or by their own aspirations for personal achievement. Nike uses those emotions to project their community of fans and athletes into a world of dreams.

CHAPTER 4
The current
state of branding:
Some trends

INTRODUCTION TO CHAPTER 4:

The trends I will discuss in this chapter are not new. We experienced them throughout 2010 and 2011, and even before. Nonetheless, here are the five prominent trends that will continue to shape the world of branding and e-marketing in the years to come.

- Companies surrender their brands to the community

- Social media becomes a mainstream affair

- Community management evolves into an essential function

- Email re-emerges

- Storytelling takes center stage

Trend: More and more, marketers will be forced to surrender their brands to an increasingly powerful community of consumers.

COMPANIES SURRENDER THEIR BRANDS
TO THE COMMUNITY

What is a brand's identity? From the perspective of a company, our brand used to be what <u>we</u> told people it was. Through our corporate communication, we played the dominant role in shaping people's opinions about our products. Today, a brand is what the <u>community decides</u> it is. In the Internet age, companies have lost much of their ability to mold customer perceptions. They must accept that branding today has become, at best, an interactive co-creation with a user community.

There simply is no choice. In today's world, **marketers are forced to surrender their brands** to the consumer community. This necessary "letting go" of the branding machinery will lead to profound changes in the way this branding game is played.

Far more than in the past, modern users of products have power and a true voice. They critique, recommend, and vilify products every day on the social sites. In numerous cases, influential bloggers have shaped public opinion about a brand more than the brand owners themselves. This is because the stories users tell will always be far more credible than the "official" communication from the company.

Increasingly, users communicate directly with each other, and it is the stories that consumers tell, the thoughts and experiences they share, that shape a brand. Today, word spreads quickly from blogger to blogger, from Twitter to Twitter, and on Facebook pages.

Brands no longer shape people's ideas. The days when companies could tell end users what to believe through creative TV ads are long gone. Increasingly, modern consumers are influenced by the comments of Facebook friends, by blogs or by online chatter, far more than by any messages they might be hearing from companies.

Consider the recent case of Pampers, Proctor and Gamble's best-selling diaper brand, with sales of about $8.5 billion worldwide in 2009, representing more than 10 per cent of total company revenues.

When P&G launched the new Dry Max version of Pampers in March 2010 in the US, official corporate communications called it the "driest and thinnest" Pampers ever, some 20 per cent lighter than its predecessor. For the launch, a traditional media campaign was accompanied by an online strategy now common in the US, with samples of the new product sent to influential bloggers in order to build grass-roots enthusiasm.

However, rather than the anticipated grass-roots approval, there was somewhat of an outcry on the blogs. "Mama" in San Diego complained in one of numerous critical reviews on Diapers.com that the product worked "like Teflon". She claimed that she had never purchased diapers that worked so poorly and concluded that she would never buy them again.

"Lib" from Arlington, Virginia, was even more incensed, commenting that her child had developed the worst case of diaper rash she ever had in just one night.

As P&G began responding to such customer complaints on an individual basis, they were simultaneously monitoring the burgeoning online concern. By early May, increasing numbers of parents were asserting that Dry Max diapers were causing horrible rashes.

Facebook pages soon appeared, with names such as "Bring back the Pampers Cruisers, Dump Dry Max", "Recall Pampers Dry Max Diapers" and "Pampers, Just Admit you made a mistake already". These pages quickly mobilized thousands of supporters, with one garnering close to 10,000 fans.

Blogging and consumer chatter continued online, mostly about such problems as severe diaper rash, infections and chemical burns. By early May, P&G knew it had no choice but to engage with the online community in new and different ways. The company began by opening lines of communication with four highly influential "blogging moms", inviting them and their children to spend a day at the company's baby care center in Cincinnati, to discuss with managers and researchers the process they use, and all the work they do, in developing a new diaper such as Dry Max.

In the longer term, the Dry Max incident is causing P&G to call into question its entire product development process, which is legendary among corporations and studied at the world's top business schools. This process was conceived and refined in the era of one-way broadcast media, and it may no longer be relevant in the rapidly-emerging age of consumer participation.

As companies inevitably come to accept the sharing of control of their brands and their product development processes, the best ones will do less traditional broadcasting. They will engage more and more in an ongoing and meaningful conversation with their consumers. In chapter 5, I discuss some of the many ways to manage, and to profit from, that conversation.

Trend: Social media has truly become a mainstream phenomenon in our society.

SOCIAL MEDIA BECOMES A MAINSTREAM AFFAIR

Of course, Facebook, Twitter and the like are not new to the marketplace, but it is in 2010-2011 that their influence reached something of a tipping point, a complete integration into our daily lives, and also into our working lives.

The impact of social media on marketing is becoming enormous. In the world of business, social media has become a widespread, ubiquitous phenomenon that no enterprise can afford to ignore. Wherever I traveled in 2010 and 2011, everyone seemed to be talking about new ways to manage and communicate in the age of "social". This tendency will certainly continue, and indeed gain momentum, in the years to come.

Social media has achieved complete integration into daily life. Anyone anywhere can broadcast anything, and messages can literally reach thousands of users in seconds. Mass movements can start almost instantly.

Today the social web is not only a first-world phenomenon. According to the Financial Times, Facebook now is used by 92 percent of the Internet population of Turkey, and 87 percent in Indonesia.

On 20 August 2010, the government of Argentina announced its intention to close the state-owned Internet service Fibertel. Within hours, angry customers had opened a Facebook page called "Say No to the Closing of Fibertel". In its first 24-hours of operation, the page amassed some 23,000 fans. Many members of the nascent "community" expressed their discontent at losing their email addresses. Others raised concerns for Internet users in remote areas of this third-world nation, consumers in places where there was thought to be no alternative service provider.

Within two days the Facebook page had gained significant momentum, with more than 60,000 fans. Participants were using both Facebook and Twitter to organize massive protest marches in cities throughout the country. Meanwhile, the government began receiving complaints on Twitter at the rate of more than one per minute.

The popular daily newspaper *Clarín* credited the "viral nature of social networks", where messages can be sent instantaneously to hundreds of friends, with creating a stir so huge that government ministers were pushed into making public statements in response to the uproar, less than 48 hours after the original announcement. By 24 August, high government officials were calling for a public investigation.

What do we learn from this Argentine anecdote? On the one hand, we should not be terribly surprised by events such as this. We read of the impact of social media every day, and we see the impressive statistics about people's participation on social sites. For example, the *Financial Times* announced in a headline on 21 June 2010 that Facebook was "on course to reach 1 billion users".

On the other hand, what happened so swiftly in Argentina might give us cause to consider how the reach, power, and impact of social media are changing our entire planet. People everywhere now have a voice, in the developed world, certainly, but also in far-flung places such as Argentina.

Intelligent use of social media allows companies to create powerful viral effects, while bypassing the more expensive traditional channels.

Today, creating online buzz can be more effective than using traditional advertising.

To understand the impact of social media for marketing, consider some recent developments in one of the most interesting marketing cases of our time, the ongoing battle between Nike and Adidas.

Adidas chose to become an official sponsor of the 2010 Football World Cup, while Nike was not. Instead, Nike focused much of its pre-tournament marketing efforts around a three minute video spot, "Write the Future". In the video, Nike stars from various countries, including Didier Drogba, Wayne Rooney and Cristiano Ronaldo, imagine and write victorious endings to the Cup. Viewers see how the World Cup might end, in success or failure, all in the mind of each of the stars.

Rather than use traditional channels, Nike chose to launch this video online. On May 22, they became the first company to do a banner block advertising blitz, using Facebook and YouTube.

By June 15, the video had been viewed more than 15 million times on YouTube. According to the *Financial Times*, it had been watched more than 29 million times on all web platforms.

The impact of an effective social media strategy was evident in the buildup to the World Cup tournament. On 11 June 2010, the English newspaper *The Guardian* reported that the Nike campaign had successfully "ambushed" the official tournament sponsors – Adidas, Coca-Cola, Visa and Sony. The online buzz created by Nike was effectively drowning out official sponsor Adidas.

Social media is forcing companies to rethink the way they communicate.

In late December 2009, Eurostar learned something about the ubiquity and the growing power of social media. On December 18, severe wintry weather in both France and Britain caused equipment failures, apparently from the difference in temperature between warm tunnels and the frigid outdoors. For the first time in Eurostar history, five trains remained stranded inside the tunnel beneath the English Channel.

Three of the trains had to be towed away, and two other trains had to be evacuated by moving all passengers onto nearby cargo trains. In spite of the efforts to remedy the situation, more than 2,000 people ended up trapped in the Channel Tunnel on Friday night, with some stuck on trains for up to 16 hours.

Many complained about the lack of supplies such as food and toilet paper, while the heat and crowded conditions led some to force open doors to get more air to breathe.

Beyond the physical challenges and discomfort, however, people complained mostly of the lack of information. Eurostar failed to provide updates in any form, on the trains, on their website, or on the social media channels. As one passenger described, "It was so frustrating, we did not have a clue what was going on."

Control your destiny, or someone else will. When we fail to communicate, clients and observers on social media will move to fill the space.

While Eurostar was failing to communicate, passengers on Twitter were "taking control" of the information space, telling others that they were stranded, describing truly unbearable conditions, and expressing complete shock at the lack of information from Eurostar.

Such tweets from angry passengers were all the more detrimental because of the absence of communication from Eurostar. In the end, Eurostar was criticized extensively on blogs, in the press and on the social sites. Some still point to this event as a watershed moment for social media. Many will remember Eurostar as the first company who completely botched up crisis management in the age of social media.

Rather than criticize Eurostar for its handling of this situation, let's focus on what they and other companies may have learned from it. Here are three quick lessons:

As social media goes mainstream, companies must be quick and transparent with information. Eurostar could have been, indeed <u>should</u> have been, communicating on all channels, in both traditional and New Age media.

Today, what people expect above all is quick and honest information. In crisis situations, acknowledge the problem, and then tell what you are doing about it. If your try to hide, or if you fail to communicate, others will tell their stories of distress, and the brand reputation will suffer more in the long term.

Sometimes, all you can do is **show people that you are there, and that you are listening.** Imagine what might have happened if Eurostar had simply published updates every hour on its website and on Twitter. In this age of mobile communication and connection on the fly, word would have spread fast. There would have been no better solution to the underlying problem, but simply being "on the air" might have made them look like a caring company, even heroes.

Social media should be about dialogue, not monologue. At the time of the crisis, Eurostar was using Twitter, but only as a "publishing" device, to announce its promotions. Ironically, as the trains were stranded in the tunnel, Eurostar was tweeting out special offers for future weekends! Today, companies are coming to understand that monitoring the community is perhaps more important than broadcasting their sales and marketing messages.

Trend: Community management is becoming a matter of top concern for a growing number of organizations.

COMMUNITY MANAGEMENT EVOLVES INTO AN ESSENTIAL FUNCTION

In a world where companies are forced to surrender their brands to the community, managing interaction with that community becomes a "mission critical" function.

Indeed, the coming years will likely see the continued emergence of the "community manager". As I traveled to conferences and clients in 2010 and 2011, I heard a good deal of discussion about exactly what a community manager's responsibilities should be, why it might be useful for an organization to have one, and the best practices for getting this job done. Increasingly, companies are coming to see the advantages of dedicating a person or a team to managing relations with its client and fan communities.

Of course, it is not the actual position of community manager that is essential, but rather the activity of managing relationships with clients, users, fans... in fact, with all stakeholders outside the company. As we explain below, companies have found various solutions for managing these relationships, with or without the community manager title. What is critical today is to realize that managing interaction with the "brand community" is becoming an increasingly vital activity for any organization.

At mydeco.com, the using of someone in the specific role of community manager turned out to be a phase. According to head of marketing Joanne Casley, the company used the post for a time, to help define their views on how to organize community management throughout their organization.

Today, community management has evolved into more of a collaborative effort, with everyone participating. As she describes: "For a time, we saw it as useful to have a community manager, to define and coordinate roles among individuals. Now, we all manage it together. Everyone tends to be very active on the site; each member of the marketing team scans the forum every day. Since we are only 35 people sitting in an open space, we can manage it all on the fly and keep everyone involved."

Sports teams tend to generate great passion among their followers, so community management can become a necessary and full-time job. At the famous Paris Saint-Germain Football Club, Julien Jalouzet monitors activity on more than 500 user websites and blogs about the team, and he leads the effort to consolidate and share fan data from various sources and departments – the website, ticketing, Internet TV, merchandizing, etc. In his view, the job of community manager has evolved into "something we simply cannot afford to live without, if we want to reach out to our fans, to understand them, and to tap into their enthusiasm."

At French kitchen equipment maker Mathon, the function of community management is also vital.

However, they see the community manager not as someone who responds directly to the community, but rather as the person responsible for filtering information, directing it to the departments or individuals concerned, and encouraging responses through the appropriate channels.

Whatever the titles and structures may be, community management appears to be an activity with a future!

Trend: Email is re-emerging as a fundamental tool for e-CRM (customer relationship management) and community management.

Email re-emerges

Of course, email has been around for a long time – since 1971 in fact – and it is not about to go away. Today, email remains the primary reason that individuals go online at home, at the office, or with their mobile devices.

Email is widely used by companies as well. Many organizations send out regular newsletters and promotional offers. Businesses use their mailing lists to do direct selling and marketing. In fact, online retailers and direct marketers have come to realize that email is the most effective channel there is for generating repeat sales from their customer lists.

In a sense, the widespread use of email hides a paradox. While everybody seems to be already using it, email remains an underexploited marketing and sales channel, and not many businesses are using its full potential. In the coming months and years, we will learn to use email as far more than a cheap and effective way to do marketing and promotion. Forward-thinking companies will make email a linchpin of their marketing and community management strategies.

Amid the recent buzz about social sites, Facebook and Twitter in particular, some seem to feel that email will diminish in importance in the coming years. At various conferences and on several occasions on my blog in 2010 and 2011, I was asked to comment on the concept that the "pull" of social media would replace the "push" of email.

To me, the emergence of social media will make effective use of email more vital, as the best organizations find innovative ways to use the two channels in harmony. In chapters 5 and 6, we will discover some of the ways that email and social can be used together for effective management of a community.

In the coming years, email will indeed re-emerge, stronger than ever, as a key component of coordinated strategies for marketing, branding and community management.

Trend: Story takes center stage.

As I travel the world today, I am truly seeing a new interest in storytelling. Business people seem to be rediscovering an age-old truth: The most effective way to make a marketing campaign interesting and relevant is to tell a good story.

STORYTELLING TAKES CENTER STAGE

As a long-time advocate of the use of storytelling in corporate communication, I am indeed encouraged these days. Wherever I go, more and more people seem to be discovering storytelling and asking how they can use it to their advantage in business. Those who are not yet using it often express a greater-than-before interest in exploring its potential. When I speak at industry conferences and trade shows, the presentations tend to draw large crowds of highly engaged participants.

In the business press as well, I have noticed that more is being written about the effective use of story in selling and marketing. In my own life, I have experienced the storytelling renewal firsthand. Since the release in October 2009 of my book about storytelling and leadership (*Les sept règles du storytelling*, Editions Pearson France, with co-author Loick Roche), I have received a veritable flood of invitations to speak at company and industry events. Storytelling in business is suddenly in vogue!

The more I talk with people in companies, the more I come to believe that **story is the missing component, the next evolution in effective corporate communication.** In other words, in the three-element strategy proposed in this book, the element that people understand the least and are perhaps using the least effectively is the art of storytelling. While we all use email, and while much of the buzz today seems to be around social media, good storytelling is the neglected part of the equation.

At the same time, something is changing today, and I sense that, in the next few years, story will truly take center stage. As we come to understand how to **exploit the power of story in combination with email and social media,** corporate storytelling will increase dramatically.

Email is most effective when it tells
a compelling story.

While I am encouraged by the growing awareness of the power of storytelling, I see few examples of companies that are using story effectively in their email messages to fans, friends and clients. When I am asked at industry events why more companies are not using the power of story in newsletters and other communication, I do not have a good answer, other than to say that I consider it a major missed opportunity.

We should learn to use storytelling more because stories give email messages <u>relevance</u>. Email that succeeds in telling a good story cuts through the clutter of our crowded daily lives. An engaging story-based message stands out from the "flood" of sales promotions, unsolicited advertisements, spam, and other uninvited guests that invade our mailboxes. When we receive an email form a company that tells good stories, we are more apt to click on it – and perhaps even enjoy the content! – rather than treat it as an intrusion in our inbox.

As we will see in chapters 5 and 6, some innovative companies <u>are</u> using storytelling in their email newsletters. They tell stories because they have come to realize that a good story is simply the best means of making an email campaign pertinent and interesting. All of these companies use campaign management software to track the success of their email campaigns, and they have discovered a simple truth: recipients are far more likely to open, click and act on an email that tells an appealing story than one that contains sales or promotional messages.

The age of social media is fast becoming the age of storytelling.

Stories are taking center stage in the digital world because **people love to share them.** What do people do on Facebook or Twitter? They share their life events, their photos, their videos, and their links to interesting stories. Then, they look for reactions, to see how many people comment on or "like" their stories. As one of my friends told me recently, "Nobody posts just to post. That's no fun at all. We post to watch the reactions to our life stories."

It has become something of a game and a challenge these days – to go out and find interesting stories and then bring them to our friends, to our "communities". Being cool in today's world is often about finding the latest, coolest things out there and being the one who sends them around.

What do organizations do with social media? They seek to grow their base of fans, to get their constituents to "like" them, to encourage people to participate in their communities. And, what brings these communities together and gives them a sense of belonging? Their stories! In fact, if we look at history, communities have always been groups who share the same stories and who find meaning in those stories. In the virtual world, just as in the physical world, communities thrive only if their stories remain relevant and interesting.

Companies are realizing more and more that their brands are only as strong as the stories people tell about them. As we will show in chapter 5, many companies are using social media, email and their websites to encourage consumers to tell stories about their experiences with a product or service. In today's world, these user-generated stories often shape brand identity more than the company's own marketing messages.

Stories will take center stage in corporate communication as companies increasingly come to realize that <u>everyone</u> can use them.

Not only are stories our most effective means of communication, they are a tool that virtually anyone can use.

Storytelling can be done on a small budget. In the bygone days of traditional marketing, building a brand usually required great resources. Content was created by expensive ad agencies, and messages were broadcast at substantial cost over television and radio airwaves.

Today, with the aid of the Internet, getting messages out is far cheaper. Through the combination of a website, a blog, an email newsletter, a Twitter account, and a social media page, we can touch large numbers of people concerned with a product or service – consumers, prospects, employees, suppliers. And, of course, the best way to <u>truly</u> touch these people is with stories, those we tell ourselves, and those we find or engender from within our community.

Storytelling can be done for virtually any product or service. When I speak at industry conferences or in companies about the virtues of storytelling, people often ask, "We don't really have stories to tell because our product, or service, is just not 'sexy'. How can <u>we</u> use storytelling?"

While I will address this issue to a greater extent in chapter 5, I can cite here the example of uSwitch.com, a free UK-based comparison and switching service that helps consumers compare prices on such everyday products and services as gas & electricity, telephone,

141

or insurance. Simon Hills, the company's Direct Marketing Manager, understands that his service is not one that generates great passion. Nonetheless, he sees storytelling as an underexploited opportunity.

In Simon's words, "Admittedly, energy switching is not the type of thing that gets customers excited. But, we have found that our clients do like to share stories of how they save money, or of what they do with the money they 'find'. They might go on a short holiday, for instance, or pay for a home improvement. To encourage these stories, we have used a combination of email and Twitter. For example, we might send out an email to encourage clients to share their successes, using our 'Tweet your saving' feature...As a company, we need to find ways to tap into storytelling more, because there are interesting stories out there."

Certainly, the phenomenal growth of Facebook in the past few years is evidence that people like to share their stories – not only their unusual, audacious or enlightening ones, but also their ordinary stories of everyday life. If uSwitch can see possibilities, so can you!

CHAPTER 5
Managing
the community

Throughout this chapter, I present ideas and arguments to demonstrate the power of combining email, social media and storytelling. I am increasingly convinced that the most effective strategies for e-marketing and for community management will be a clever mix of these three elements.

As we will see in the individual sections of this chapter, it is becoming increasingly important to use modern communication channels for listening, not just for blasting out our messages. While email and social media provide inexpensive ways to reach vast numbers of customers and prospects, we must learn to use their other capabilities as well, in particular the possibilities these channels provide for deepening our understanding of our followers and potential clients.

In customer relationships, the new world order is about community and conversation. We should no longer be asking ourselves how we can reach customers or prospects with our sales and marketing messages. A more appropriate question for today is: How can we use the entire spectrum of communication technology to aid us in creating meaningful and ongoing conversations with our community?

As social media becomes a mainstream phenomenon, as we become better at using the full potential of email, and as we progress as listeners and storytellers, we will move away from the marketer-centric approaches of the past, and toward ever more customer-centric approaches. We should embrace this profound change, as it is already happening, and because it will inevitably continue. For those who navigate it well, this sea change will bring enormous opportunity.

To begin this chapter on managing the community, my first recommendation is a simple one: Take the time to reflect and plan before jumping on the e-bandwagon. In other words, develop a comprehensive strategy.

"

"Without goals, and plans to reach them, you are like a ship that has set sail with no destination."

Fitzhugh Dodson, child psychologist

"

Make managing the community a broad-based strategic initiative

Go in with a plan. Email and social media provide the ability to reach thousands of people at very low cost, and this ability is available to everyone, including the smallest of businesses. At the same time, one of the dangers of jumping into e-marketing and social CRM is that many companies are doing it simply "because we have to be there". When everyone around us, including our competitors, seems to be blasting out emails, using fan pages on Facebook, and Tweeting out their latest news, it is easy to feel left behind.

Of course, many companies are using social media and email in their daily work, but I see relatively few who are using these tools optimally. A great number of organizations are simply pushing out their promotional messages, or trying to send "cool stuff" to impress their friends and prospects. As we will see in the various sections of this chapter, by mastering the communication tools of the Internet, we can learn to listen better, to use email and story more effectively, and to inspire a wider user base to participate in our community.

Going in with a plan means developing a broad-based perspective and a comprehensive strategy for interacting with the user community. Our plan should include clear views about the image we wish to project, how we propose to exploit the various communication platforms, and how we will organize our community management efforts internally. Take the time to have a strategic outlook, to engage the organization, and to write guidelines for employees.

In developing your e-commerce strategy, here are **some things to think about:**

Stay focused on what you seek to accomplish. Today, there are many conversations out there, on a multitude of channels. At times, it is easy to get distracted by the excitement, and then rush to be everywhere. Rather than try to be omnipresent, take the time to define your goals and to be selective about which conversations can really help you reach those goals.

Go beyond blasting and selling. The communication resources available today open new worlds of possibility for interaction with a group of followers. Making optimal use of these tools for true interaction involves a change of mindset: learning to think of them as **conversation tools** rather than just promotion and transaction tools.

Don't collect "fans". While it is easy and convenient to measure success in terms of numbers – the size of an email list or the number of fans on a Facebook page, for example – we should not necessarily be impressed by sheer quantity. Thinking strategically about e-commerce involves focusing on the **quality of the conversations** rather than only on the quantity.

Don't just monitor; learn to interact. With the growth of social media in recent years, forward-thinking organizations learned to listen to the "buzz" on the Internet, to see what was being said about them. Today, there is a growing expectation that companies will interact online, using the channels that clients are using. Smart businesses are seeing the advantages of finding creative ways to engage with their target audience in live conversations.

Write unambiguous guidelines for employees, or better yet <u>with</u> the employees, about what online activities are appropriate. Since the Internet is an open forum, employees may post their own statements, or respond to online chatter, at will. Whether they participate personally or in the context of work, all members of an organization should share an understanding of the ways they should be involved – what is encouraged, what is condoned, and what may be viewed as unsuitable behavior.

While a lengthy discussion of this topic is beyond the scope of this book, I am certain that many readers have seen the numerous YouTube videos or Facebook posts which have led to the disciplining or firing of employees for actions offensive to their employers.

Don't wait for a crisis. As some of the examples in this book demonstrate, negative blog posts, YouTube videos or retweets about an incident can damage a brand's reputation quickly. Rather than react when negative news hits, learn to be strategic and proactive in maintaining your e-reputation.

Don't outsource the conversation. With the growth of Internet marketing, email and social media, numerous consulting companies have sprung up to help organizations manage their brand conversations and their online reputations. While outside advisors may be useful for planning a strategy and for guiding implementation, there is simply no substitute for having your own conversations with your own community. My view is that these conversations are too important to outsource, and that you will be best served if you develop the necessary competencies within the organization to take charge of your Internet communication. **Don't hire a conversation company. Become a conversation company!**

"In order to speak, one must first listen,
learn to speak by listening."

Rumi, 13th century Persian poet

DEVELOP THE MINDSET OF A SOCIAL ANTHROPOLOGIST

Changing the focus from product to people: In the past, we were broadcasters, and our brands shouted their messages to consumers. The process started with a product, and companies defined the images they wanted to create around the product. Today, consumers talk directly to each other through the medium of the Internet. Our brands are shaped by the impressions, the experiences and the stories that these highly connected individuals are sharing with each other, independent of us.

As I discussed in a section of chapter 4 on "marketers surrendering their brands to the community", we no longer tell the world what our brand stands for. Rather, consumers tell each other – and us – what our brands symbolize to the world.

I believe we are at a watershed moment in marketing communication. Advertisers and marketers are just beginning to come to grips with how digital media has already changed, and will continue to change, the very nature of interaction with customers and prospects. Nowadays, we cannot start with our product or with our message around the product. We must learn to begin by studying the human beings who are our potential consumers.

From brand management to anthropology, and from broadcasting to listening: Changes in terminology, and in job titles, can be quite revealing. These days, as I talk to companies, my impression is that the era of the "brand manager" is giving way to the era of the "community manager". Yesterday we managed brands. Today, we will be far more successful if we learn to be social anthropologists.

What is the mindset of social anthropologists, and how do they spend their time? Mostly, they pay attention, they watch, and they learn. Social anthropologists show a true interest in studying the behavior of communities. They ask lots of questions. Above all, they listen far more than they speak.

The advice of a 13th century Persian poet is indeed timeless: we must learn to speak by listening.

More on how to do this in the next section…

66

"Somebody is out there talking about you, perhaps more than you realize. In today's world, it is crucial that you know what they are saying, and it is becoming equally crucial that you learn to talk with them as well...It is important that you treat them as equals and that you are authentic and transparent in your conversations."

Dr. Johann Fuller, CEO HYVE AG
Assistant Professor, University of Innsbruck
Research Affiliate, Sloan School of Management MIT

99

LEARN TO USE MULTIPLE CHANNELS INTELLIGENTLY

With our mindset of social anthropologists, we should be using all the tools of the Internet, to listen to, understand, and truly engage our communities.

Unfortunately, a great number of organizations today are falling into the trap of simply using the new channels in old familiar ways. In other words, they are still communicating by sending out their promotional messages; the only difference is that they are broadcasting using the "trendy" new media. We first saw this phenomenon in the 1990s with email, when many direct marketers simply transported their blasting of sales messages to the new medium, ignoring the vast potential of email for engaging clients in a conversation.

In more recent times, we have witnessed a failure to exploit the true potential of social media, even on the part of some intelligent, market savvy people and companies. For example, a 2010 article in *Fast Company* chided US President Barack Obama for using social media as "just another platform for press releases, rather than a way for followers (and potential voters) to gain direct access."

As we saw in the Eurostar incident in chapter 4, the company's failure to communicate with its stranded customers during a crisis, and its use of Twitter at the same moment to advertise future promotions, led to a public relations disaster.

What brands such as Eurostar and Barack Obama failed to understand is that the advent of social media represents an opportunity to completely rethink the ways we communicate. Rather than simply getting "out there" with our traditional-style messages, we should be looking for innovative ways to tap into the power of the new media.

So, how can we learn to use these new media as more than mere broadcast channels? Here are a few thoughts:

First, monitor the conversations. The world of social media is ever-evolving. While sites such as Twitter, Facebook and YouTube have a strong following today, users can change habits – and platforms – quickly. A company, particularly a small one with limited resources, cannot be everywhere on the Internet. However, one <u>can</u> **monitor the ongoing online conversations** to make intelligent decisions about where to be and how to be there.

There are numerous software programs, both free and paid, that can help monitor "buzz" and alert you when your keywords are mentioned on the Internet. Of course, you should want to listen to anything being said directly about you, or about your core business activities. **Following keywords** can provide insight about who your customers and prospects are and what they are concerned about. Listening in on a wide variety of channels will also allow you to identify dissatisfied customers, and it may even help you avert a budding crisis.

Another way to find out where you should be listening is to **survey your customers** about their Internet behavior. What social sites are they on? What blogs do they read? What websites do they visit regularly? What issues are they following? Your clients' answers to such questions will help you see more clearly which platforms and company websites you should be monitoring. It will help you **identify key bloggers and influential individuals** with whom you might consider building relationships. In addition, surveying your customers will help you tailor your own messages, by focusing on the themes that interest them most.

Second, engage with people where <u>they</u> are. As you learn more about where your customers and prospects are, and what is important to them, you will be more able to engage them where they are. When I say "where they are", you should read this in two ways: first, engage them **on the channels** they are using, and second, engage them **on matters** they care about.

Careful listening to the universe of social media will uncover insight about what types of messages will resonate with your target audience, and such information will help in all your communication, particularly email. In the past few years, one complaint I have heard over and over from companies is that "open rates" on their emailing are going down. The "email overload" that most of us are experiencing today leads people to swiftly delete things that are not perceived as relevant. We can use monitoring of the social channels to segment our markets, and to meet our target audience where <u>they</u> are with messages that are <u>pertinent</u> to them.

While monitoring and finding ways to engage with an audience are a necessity today, tomorrow they will not be sufficient. One of the great advantages of our increasingly connected world is the ability to talk with our followers in real time. As such, we should be looking continuously for new and meaningful ways to interact with people online.

Third, find innovative and meaningful ways to interact with your audience. President Obama's use of email and social media to issue press releases has not played well with his constituents because people simply want more. Today, consumers do not want to be passive recipients. They want to be actively involved. They want to give feedback. They expect more than mere information; they expect a conversation.

Modern voters will increasingly expect public officials to engage them in a continuous process and to give them a voice. As the *Fast Company* article advises, "The key is making sure people... are making an authentic impact on the process. We must apply these lessons to other activities in the future: incorporating audiences into bill crafting, oversight, hearings, committee meetings, floor activities – make the public's interaction real." In much the same way, clients of businesses will seek a true dialogue with the company, to have their voice in product development, to comment on service policies, or to suggest website content, for example.

One company using social media to engage their fans and prospects in a meaningful dialogue is mydeco. com. Joanne Casley describes what they do: "We decided to go after people where they are, to identify the conversations and the passion around design, and to grow our presence where those conversations are taking place. There are also lots of bloggers about design, and we follow those. We follow tweets around certain keywords. Who is talking about interior design, and why? Then, we follow them. If people use Twitter to question, 'Where can I find red velvet curtains?', for example, then we try to tweet back to them, and we continue the conversation. We also reply on Facebook, if that's where the question comes from."

How is the use of channels evolving in business? Some industry pundits are predicting a veritable explosion in the commercial uses of social media. Nick Heys, founder and CEO of Emailvision, predicts that we will see increased corporate presence on social channels, and development of new ways to use them, in particular for sales and tracking. He points to the example of forward-thinking companies such as Dell and Lush, who already generate significant percentages of their revenues from social media, particularly Twitter and Facebook. Additionally, Nick thinks we will see an increasing number of software tools and services that measure the impact of social media. As he comments, "I think we will see the emergence of Facebook or other social sites as standalone direct marketing channels-representing an additional and complementary source of business for companies. And, of course, marketers will want to quantify results, for example to gauge the impact of a Facebook post for creating traffic and generating sales... just as we measure results of our email campaigns today."

"

"If you want to play in the community arena, you're going to have to give up some of that control, and take the good, the bad and the crazy that comes along with it."

Heather Champ, former community manager, Flickr

"

Accept loss of control

Let's begin this section with two short anecdotes:

<u>United and the Guitar</u>: When United Airlines broke Dave Carroll's $3500 guitar in March 2008, the incident quickly grew far bigger than the company could ever have imagined. In fact, what started out as simple customer complaint was destined to become something of a cult incident. Carroll initially filed a grievance asking for compensation, using the normal customer complaint channels. United's lack of response for nine months led the Canadian artist to record a song – and YouTube music video – called "United Breaks Guitars", which he released on July 6, 2009.

The tune and film turned rapidly into something of a viral phenomenon. Within 3 days of its release, the video had been viewed 466,000 times on YouTube. The song hit number one on the iTunes Music Store in its first week on the market. Coverage of Carroll's lament spilled over to traditional media; among others, CNN and the BBC reported the song's instant success and the embarrassment it was causing United. In December 2009, *Time* magazine named "United Breaks Guitars" #7 on its list of the Top 10 Viral Videos for 2009. By August 2010, the video had been seen more than 9 million times!

For the airline, it was a true customer service and public relations disaster. But, the company did end up learning from the debacle. The broken guitar episode incited top management to make certain changes. Today, United uses Carroll's video as part of its training program for customer service employees.

Nestlé and the Palm Oil Controversy: In March 2010, Greenpeace posted a video on YouTube, asserting that Nestlé's popular Kit Kat bar contained palm oil produced in areas where rain forests had been destroyed. Nestlé responded swiftly, forcing removal of the video for alleged copyright violations.

Instead of silencing criticism and ending the chapter, Nestlé's reaction led to a guerilla campaign against the company. Greenpeace reposted the clip on other websites, used Twitter to spread the word of Nestlé's "censored" video, and told users where they could find it. Outraged individuals, including some partisans of Greenpeace and some others, joined a movement to post angry messages on Nestlé's Facebook page, substituting the word Killer for Kit Kat. Various anti-Nestlé groups also took up the cause.

Within a few months, Nestlé was forced to give in to Greenpeace's demands, announcing in May that they would rid their supply chain of any sources involved in the destruction of rainforests.

What are some of the lessons of these two anecdotes? Let's focus on a few.

First of all, companies can no longer hide. In these times, it can be quite dangerous to ignore negative comments from customers. Before the Internet and the advent of social media, a complaint such as Dave Carroll's against United Airlines would have been handled privately, between company and consumer. Increasingly in today's world, matters like these can become items open to the public, and the publicity from a single incident can cause incalculable damage to a company's image. If your company is perceived as having poor customer service, people will know, their friends will know, their tribes will know, word will spread, and your reputation will suffer. In today's connected world, there is simply nowhere to hide.

On the one hand, having nowhere to hide can make a company feel naked and vulnerable. Today, even powerful multinationals may be exposed to mass movements created on the Internet; such movements were simply not possible a few short years ago.

On the other hand, operating in a world of openness where no one can hide may be seen as an opportunity to build your brand and your story. If your product or service is outstanding, your customers now have the power to let the world know.

Second, we can no longer control the flow of information. Nestlé thought they could stop the showing of a video they deemed detrimental to the company's reputation. While such an approach may have worked in the past, it is far less possible in today's environment of openness and free flowing information. In a world where individuals can share their concerns virtually, publish almost anything freely, and mobilize groups rapidly around a cause, trying to cover up your secrets may increase public resentment against you.

Third, it pays to be transparent. If your story is authentic, you should welcome transparency and let it work to your advantage. For example, if you claim to provide great customer service, and then really do it, interested people will talk about you – on social sites and on blogs.

In chapter 4, I stated that marketers today are surrendering their brands to an increasingly powerful community of consumers. In essence, what this community of consumers is saying about you has become more important than what you are broadcasting about yourself.

Forward-thinking organizations are coming to view this loss of control over the brand message as an opportunity. If your own messages are clear and authentic, if the experience you provide to consumers is first-rate, let others speak for you. Let them tell their stories. Let transparency work for you!

An example of an organization that uses transparency to its advantage is French kitchenware maker Mathon, a company we will examine in more detail in later sections of this chapter. When customers ask questions or make complaints on Mathon's Facebook page, someone from the company responds directly on the page. Thus, Mathon's customer service practices are there for the world to see; clients and prospects can reach their own conclusions about Mathon, the quality of its products, and its approach to service.

Yoann Le Berrigaud, director of e-commerce at Mathon, speaks openly about transparency and loss of control. As he proclaims: "It is important to speak up, and to allow your customers to do the same. This is risky; letting customers speak freely can make one feel naked and vulnerable. But it also allows us to position ourselves, on Facebook for example, as a company that organizes a truly open community around its brand. It allows us to truly build trust with our customers."

"When we started our company, we thought we should communicate as much as possible. We wanted to be on all the available channels, and to have big lists of fans. Over time, we came to realize that the number of people we communicate with is not as important as their level of involvement. For us, it has proven more effective to communicate less often, and with a smaller group of followers, but a group that truly shares our vision and goals...Today, we focus on having meaningful conversations more than on having numerous ones."

Hans Christian Wilson,
founder of High and Low Adventure Park,
and award-winning Norwegian entrepreneur

SET CLEAR GOALS AND USE NEW METRICS

In May 2010, I read that Dunkin' Donuts had 80% fewer followers on Facebook and Twitter than Starbucks. That single number would lead one to believe that Starbucks has been more successful than its rival in social media activity. But, if we dig a bit deeper into the story, we find that Dunkin' Donuts may have fans that are more valuable to the brand. For example, a study from the same time period revealed that a Dunkin' Donuts partisan is 35% more likely than a Starbucks follower to recommend the company to his friends.

My purpose in citing these statistics is not to criticize Starbucks or praise Dunkin' Donuts. Rather, I put forward this case to highlight the point that a simple look at numbers often does not tell the entire story.

Take the example of email. As we all know, a company might have a massive email list, but many individuals on that list may be passive recipients who generate little activity. Another company with a far smaller list may be more effective at mining data, engaging and targeting their customers, and sending relevant content that leads directly to sales.

It is much the same with social media. Simply having a large number of followers on Twitter, or a sizeable Facebook "community" does not guarantee results, either in terms of sales or positive impact to brands.

What does make a difference is <u>engagement</u>, but that is a notion that can be hard to measure. As social media becomes increasingly pervasive, we must develop new metrics that focus on the <u>activities</u> of our fans rather than on their sheer numbers.

In the world of e-marketing, we must learn to look at a combination of old, traditional metrics – such as new customers or purchases generated – and some newer soft metrics, such as our e-reputation and the "social value" of our brands. One emerging concept today is the notion of "social currency", which attempts to measure a company's ability to engage stakeholders as partners in growth and sustainability. Though difficult to compute in terms of return on investment, growing our social currency and online reputation will create substantial value in the longer term.

We need to find – or invent – new measures that focus on the quality of conversations rather than just their quantity. We should look for ways to gauge levels of fan engagement and influence. What tools can help us calculate these things? Increasingly, companies will want to know.

Numerous companies have commented to me that they are hesitant to make major investments in a social media strategy because the returns on such investments are not measurable. And I must admit, determining the economic impact of social media activity has proven tricky, to say the least. As opposed to email, where tracking tools have become increasingly refined, results of a company's social media efforts remain difficult to calculate.

In their email marketing campaigns, smart companies have learned the value of watching closely what people are actually <u>doing</u> when they receive newsletters or other email messages. Who is opening them, acting on them, visiting the website to purchase, or forwarding them to others? Measuring this activity can identify not only the most active clients, but also the most enthusiastic fans of a brand, for example those who regularly forward emails to large numbers of friends.

Social media opens up a vast new world in marketing because it lets anybody talk to everybody. For the first time, consumers can talk about brands with their friends, and even with the entire world. The dynamic of "friends-telling-friends" has enormous potential for brand building; it is word-of-mouth with massive scale.

Thus far, however, companies seem to have more questions than answers when it comes to putting a value on most social media transactions. For instance, what is the worth to our brand of an individual follower on Facebook or Twitter, particularly one with a large

171

following himself? Can one assign a value to the "buzz" that an active fan creates around the brand? Or, what is the return on investment of a banner ad or an email promotion that nets numerous Facebook followers but few actual purchases?

While firms struggle to put a value on their social media activity, software companies continue to build tools to track the social behavior of consumers. As these tools evolve, and as we become more adept at studying the behavior of the members of our communities, here are some of the things we can do:

Define our goals. Of course, finding things to measure is not particularly difficult. We can look at the size of our email list, the number of people who "like" us on Facebook, the number of people following on Twitter, or the number of views of our YouTube videos. Unfortunately, these convenient metrics tell us only about volume, not about activity or engagement.

Ultimately, we need to do some hard and clear thinking about our business objectives and about which metrics might help us reach those objectives. Are we engaged in Internet marketing principally to generate revenue, to increase customer satisfaction, to lower our marketing costs, or to build an e-reputation? Before we can look to evaluate our successes and failures, we need to have a clear idea of why we are engaged in e-marketing and what we want out of it.

Consider the quality of conversations, not just the quantity. Once we have articulated our goals, we should look to identify and join the conversations that will help us reach them. So, rather than watch our numbers of followers, we will increasingly seek to assess the influence of individuals, their sense of connection to our brand, sense of community, and level of advocacy. Who are key individuals of our brand community, and how can we improve the quality of our conversations with *these* people in particular?

We have to measure our success not by how many people receive our message, but by how many people find it *relevant and worth sharing*, exciting enough to comment on and to pass along to their tribes.

At the Paris Saint-Germain football club, community manager Julien Jalouzet expresses it this way: "With email and social media, we find that the traditional measures – reach, awareness, and frequency of message – are only a small part of the story. We *know* we can reach large numbers of people. Now we want to see if our content is getting to the *right* people, if it is *speaking* to them, and if they are *sharing* it."

Map user engagement and activity. Not only do we want to be in the right conversations, we want to develop an understanding of what people are doing in these conversations. And, since we want to engage the community with content that is <u>relevant</u> and <u>worthy of sharing</u>, our metrics should focus on these two elements to determine whether or not we are progressing toward

173

our goal. Some of these metrics I will discuss here are non-traditional and a bit difficult to quantify today, but tools for measuring them are evolving constantly. To help us see if our messages are resonating with our target audience, we should watch:

- Level of activity in the community: Numerous measures are possible. For example, what is the ratio of active members to total members? Is this ratio rising or falling? Do individual visitors tend to be active on multiple touch points (website, blog, social pages, etc.)? Are comments on our blog increasing?

- Stickiness: On average, what is the length of engagement with our content? In other words, how long do visitors stay on our website or our Facebook page? Is the time people spend with us increasing or decreasing?

- Conversion rates: How often are we turning visitors into subscribers to newsletters or purchasers of services?

- Multiplying of messages: When people repeat our messages, how quickly and how widely do they spread? When social members share, do their networks then re-share? How soon and how often? How many "friends of friends" are we attracting to the community?

When Dunkin' Donuts organizes an online contest where clients send in photos of themselves drinking product, they track not only the number of participants but also the "product plugs" generated by the posts and status updates that people put on the social sites. In

2010, one such online event produced nearly 4 million of these plugs.

Bring influencers into our conversations. Another question we should ask is, "how successful are we at engaging the individuals who appear to be leaders of the conversations?" One of the benefits of social media is that it allows us to eavesdrop on the marketplace, to listen to what our target audience is saying, and to identify the key individuals who have the most influence in the online conversations.

Companies such as mydeco.com and Paris Saint-Germain monitor the bloggers and follow the keywords related to their core activities. In that way, they can reach out to key people, make special offers to them, even meet with them, and try to involve them in the company's endeavors.

The now famous Old Spice video project cited in chapter 2 was so successful because of who they were able to engage in the online conversation. As questions and suggestions came in, the social media team and scriptwriters sought to create viral effects by "looking at who's written those comments, what their influence is and what comments have the most potential for helping us create new content."

Turn fans into advocates. While it is easy to get people to "like" something, it is far more difficult to get them to advocate for it. More than having lots of fans, our goal should be to turn our followers into brand evangelists.

As the opening example from this section makes clear, Starbucks beats Dunkin' Donuts in number of fans but loses when it comes to customer advocacy. This is because Dunkin focuses on involving its followers in more active ways.

Dunkin's director of interactive and relationship marketing, David Tryder, explains that company promotions are built around the goal of turning fans into online celebrities. For example, each week they choose a different fan photo to be the official Facebook profile picture. Or, they disseminate user-generated snapshots of people drinking Dunkin' Donuts coffee in atypical situations.

Far more than its rival, Dunkin' has succeeded in giving fans a sense of belonging to a community, and at turning them into true promoters of the brand. Their engagement-based initiatives help explain why people are 50% more likely to have heard good things about Dunkin' Donuts than about Starbucks.

"

"I see myself as an organizer and facilitator of the community around the brand."

Yoann Le Berrigaud, director of e-commerce, Mathon

"

TREAT COMMUNITY MANAGEMENT AS
A PROCESS OF RELATIONSHIP BUILDING

French kitchenware maker Mathon is a surprising company. When Yoann Le Berrigaud, director of e-commerce, speaks at e-marketing forums, almost nobody in the audience has heard of his company. So, he introduces himself with a question and a statement:

- "Ok, you may not know much about Mathon, but how many of you use pots and pans?" (Of course, nearly everyone raises a hand.)

- "Well, I sell pots and pans."

Now, one would think that a business that makes its living selling pots and pans would not necessarily be doing much to foster an online user community. But, if one visits Mathon's Facebook page, one quickly gets the impression that this group of some 50,000 fans (as of December 2011) is literally buzzing with activity.

So, how does a company with an unglamorous product that we use in our daily lives develop such a following? First, they make quality products that people enjoy using. And second, they develop a coherent e-marketing program that uses a combination of email, social media and storytelling to build meaningful relationships with their clients and prospects.

Let's take a closer look at some of the things Mathon does and see what we might learn about community management and relationship building.

Use passion points to cultivate a sense of belonging. Communities come together around a shared passion. In the case of Mathon, the product itself is not one that many people are passionate about, so they looked to a related activity: cooking. On their Facebook page, they publish recipes and the stories around them, their origins, their histories and their variations.

When a recipe is posted, members of the community react, perhaps with the story of a childhood memory that the recipe has triggered, or perhaps with a different story of how the dish is prepared in their restaurant, or in their family kitchen. The page stays lively because the company enables members of the community to connect, interact and share their enthusiasm with other like-minded individuals.

Don't dominate the conversation. Facilitate it. Yoann Le Berrigaud, Mathon's director of e-commerce, does not see himself as spokesperson for the brand, but rather as the "organizer and facilitator" of the community around the brand.

For many companies, becoming a facilitator and "letting go" of the conversation involves a change of mindset, one that can be difficult. Our more traditional companies still communicate by broadcasting their brand messages to the world, and they still fear loss of control. However, and as we have seen in chapter 4, forward-thinking companies understand that a brand today is what the user community tells us it is. The best we can do now is to provide a space and a forum for users to interact.

So, don't seek to control the community. Don't try to create the community in your image, or around your messages. Create it for the users. If you build it around the passion points of the members, they will come, and they will contribute.

Use email and social media to build trust. Many businesses today use their websites and email lists for direct sales, and this can of course be quite effective. At the same time, forward-thinking companies nurture their online communities in ways that are not sales oriented.

Mathon uses its email list and Facebook page together in a program of "prospect relationship management". First, they send emails that encourage people to sign up as fans on the Facebook page. Then, they use this page to rally their core audience around the brand. They seek to provide meaningful exchanges that give users a sense of partnership with the company, as well as a sense of belonging to the group.

One of the ways that Mathon fosters trust is by employing the various communication channels for distinct purposes. Email is primarily for maintaining contact, Facebook for creating excitement in the community, and the website for selling. Thus, on the Facebook page, there are no sales messages, no promotions or advertising; it is mostly about maintaining a lively conversation and letting participants tell their stories. Users can enjoy the interaction without feeling the pressure to purchase.

Relationship building helps us understand our customers. If one follows the conversations on Mathon's Facebook page, one realizes that the user comments are an increasingly important resource for discovering what is on their target users' minds. In fact, on any active social media page, individuals reveal themselves in a forum that anyone can monitor.

Many corporations are discovering that social media is a rich source of market information. By listening in to online conversations and by using today's analytical tools, businesses have the resources to identify potential customers, and to gain insight into their buying habits and activity – things that in the past could be done only with expensive research. The more companies engage in meaningful relationships and conversations with users, the better this information will be.

In the future, relationships with our brand communities will be even more intimate, and thus more valuable. Much as users today "opt-in" to receive email from organizations, tomorrow's consumers will enter into conversations with companies they trust, giving these companies permission to get to know them by following their clicks, or by authorizing them to send personalized promotional offers. Users will also be able to share elements of their personal profiles, such as the list of companies they "like" or their lists of friends.

The more consumers feel respect and trust in their relationship with our company, the more they will assist us in knowing them and understanding their behavior.

The process of relationship building will also increase sales. As the case of Mathon demonstrates, it can be quite effective to create a user forum that is separate from the sales channels. Today, many consumers are tired of the constant torrent of advertising and promotional messages on websites, in email and on social media sites. These people often appreciate a company's willingness to have meaningful exchanges with them before engaging in a selling process.

So, one of your goals should be to get your prospects into a conversation that feels like a partnership, an ongoing dialogue that will keep you "top of mind" for them. To this end, email and social media can work hand in hand because they allow you to stay connected on multiple touch points, and to cultivate meaningful relationships over time. Then, when the people you have been talking to are interested in making a purchase, there is a good chance that they will turn to you and say, "Ok, we're ready to buy; I really like what these people are about, so let's talk to them".

"Even with the advent of social media, email will remain the workhorse of the system. It is the most profitable sales channel that has ever existed, and it will continue to be so.**"**

Nick Heys, founder and CEO, Emailvision

"

TAP INTO THE TRUE POTENTIAL OF EMAIL

Email remains an underexploited channel: As we noted in chapter 4, reports of email's demise are greatly exaggerated! If anything, email is taking on greater importance today, as more and more organizations learn of the central role it can play in managing a community.

In my travel and interviewing of the past 12 months, here is one of my somewhat surprising discoveries: While social media sites may be the glamorous or trendy channel today, email is the linchpin of the customer relationship strategy of many an enterprise.

Despite all the rush and the current fashion to use social media, many companies I spoke with are coming to see email as the most important way to stay in touch with their clients and prospects. The experience of Julien Jalouzet, who manages relations with the fan community at the Paris Saint-Germain (PSG) football club, is typical. As he states, these days it is quite easy to get people to "become a fan" on Facebook. They merely click a button, and they may still have a very low level of engagement with the team.

As Julien describes, one of the major objectives of their Facebook page is to find ways to get email addresses and to begin communicating with fans directly. From the Facebook page, the team runs contests with prizes. For example, they might ask participants to answer a question and give an email address, in order to be eligible for free tickets for the next weekend's match. Once they have a fan's email address, and only then, can a company like the PSG begin a process of converting the individual into a customer.

Email will increasingly be used for qualifying, learning about and targeting customers: Nick Heys of Emailvision calls email "the workhorse of sales". As Emailvision's clients have seen for more than ten years, regular email campaigns and newsletters produce consistent – and sometimes dramatic – increases in sales and profits. The future, Nick says, will be about delving further into email's potential in the customer relationship process.

If we learn to take advantage of tracking tools, every email marketing campaign provides an outstanding opportunity to learn more about one's customers. As Nick points out, "Every time you send out a campaign, you can add to your goldmine of learning. You can track which customers open and act on your offers and which ones don't. Over time, you can identify your most frequent customers and see which ones spend the most. Then, you can segment your list and build a tailored strategy and story for targeting each type of customer."

Henry Ford once famously commented that if he had asked his customers what they wanted before he conceived the Model T automobile, "they'd have asked for a faster horse". One of the coolest things about email is that you can test new offers, new pricing, new creative approaches, new products, new anything – stuff that your customers never knew they wanted.

Forward-thinking marketers are starting to use new email testing tools to identify marketing "breakthroughs" that they can roll out on all their sales and marketing channels. Again, to quote industry maven Nick Heys, "Marketing software companies now provide outstanding testing and tracking tools to use with campaigns, for example A/B split and multivariate testing tools which measure the impact and success of new ideas almost instantaneously, allowing marketers to identify and roll out a winning offer quickly."

Email in concert with social media and storytelling: Companies are discovering innovative and powerful ways to combine social media, email and storytelling to network with their communities. The interaction of a company's email list and Facebook page, for example, can extend its communication reach in remarkable ways.

When Mathon wanted to grow its Facebook community, they used a friendly email that encouraged all their contacts to become "fans". The response was overwhelming. In the 48 hours following the email campaign, they had acquired ten thousand new followers on their page, as well as hundreds of comments from individuals thanking the company for reaching out to them.

Once a social community is alive and thriving, people love to share their content. On Mathon's site and

Facebook page, for example, people share their recipes, their pictures of cakes or other masterpieces, their cooking advice, or innovative ideas for using, fixing and cleaning kitchen equipment.

Of course, what active users of a community do on the social pages or on the company website leads to extensive storytelling. People simply <u>love</u> to share their stories – experiences, successes, or even amusing mishaps – with other interested parties. Many companies today are coming to see the power of sharing these user stories, whether in newsletters or by pointing them out on the site and encouraging visitors to read or watch them.

At many of the companies I interviewed, I sensed a good deal of surprise at the level of involvement of their users. Such was certainly the case at Filofax, the UK-based maker of stylish, leather-bound personal organizers. While the company always knew they had a loyal following, group marketing manager Jessica Stephens once commented to me that she and her colleagues were often amazed by the depth of emotion – even fanaticism – that they found in the storytelling of their customers.

Create a virtuous cycle of customer participation: In active communities, email, social media and storytelling often work in synergy. Stories of members provide fodder for the social sites, activity on the social sites feeds email lists, and email campaigns generate increasing numbers of followers, who bring more user stories.

Content supplied by community members enlivens the company's email campaigns, since these user stories are far more engaging and credible than other types of corporate messages, promotional announcements or marketing campaigns. There is simply no better way to engage prospects and clients than storytelling among avid users. As user stories make the company's newsletters more vibrant and appealing, they will be shared and forwarded more frequently, inciting new members to join the community.

In turn, a Facebook or other social page can feed a company's mailing list. Through sign-up forms, through exclusive giveaways, and through users recommending the page to their friends, companies grow their contact lists. In addition, email addresses gleaned from social sites and friends carry an added benefit. Any contacts drawn from on-line sign-up sheets or user recommendations tend to be more "qualified" and interested than names drawn from purchased email lists or other sources. All of these contacts have "opted in" or have been pre-screened by a member of the community.

"A great brand is a story that's never completely told. Stories create the emotional context people need to locate themselves in a larger experience."

Scott Bedbury, *New Brand World: Eight Principles for Achieving Brand Leadership in the 21st Century*

PROVIDE STORIES TO THE COMMUNITY

Since a brand today is defined by the stories the community tells about it, and since a brand's story is an ongoing co-creation, the next three sections focus directly on the role of storytelling in managing a community. In the current segment, I discuss the importance of providing stories to the community. Then, in the next section, I advocate engaging members of the community as active participants in the storytelling process. Finally, in the last part of this chapter, I advance the concept of making your promoters and true believers – in other words, your best storytellers – part of your Hero's Journey.

The new world order is about community. We use Facebook and Twitter to connect to our friends, to our fans, to our online communities, to our "tribes". Bloggers with a following create their communities. For a brand, it is the same. The "fans" of Nike, or Coca-Cola, or IKEA constitute a community.

As the notion of an online community becomes pervasive in our world, storytelling takes on greater importance. What was true for traditional societies, where people sat around campfires to tell their stories, remains true today: Shared stories are the foundation of any tribe or community.

Telling stories is the best way to create and foster a community. Communities are collections of individuals who unite around a shared passion. Stories provide the sense of belonging, and the sense of meaning, that bind the community together. More than any other form of communication, stories have the power to inspire.

Since stories speak to our emotion, to our hearts as well as to our minds, they are the best way to express our passion.

A good story is one that provides a sense of possibility. Users should "see" themselves in your stories. mydeco.com, who call themselves the "one-stop-shop for a home as stylish as you are", state that they will help us find "inspiring interior design ideas". They do this with a website, an email newsletter, a blog, and a Facebook page. In the "Meet our Designers" section of their website, they tell the stories of celebrity designers and show rooms that these designers have decorated. In addition, they have an active blog where they tell stories of innovative concepts they are seeing at design shows and conferences, and they explain how readers might use them.

Joanne Casley, who is responsible for branding, tactical marketing and email marketing at mydeco.com, says that they use email as an effective means of providing stories to their community. In addition to sending out their weekly newsletter, every two weeks they send out an additional message, focused on a theme, where members of staff choose products and tell stories of how they can be used.

The goal of this storytelling, from famous designers and also from company staffers, is to encourage their readers to discover and dream. They seek to give their fans innovative ideas that they can put into action, to have members of their community think, "I could see myself decorating my house that way."

One of the things I like about mydeco.com's storytelling is its authenticity. They tell us that they will "inspire" us with design ideas, and the genuine stories they offer us lend enormous credibility to this claim.

Stories build trust. It is a natural human tendency. When a company or an individual tries to sell us something or convince us of something, we are suspicious. We want to push the message away. On the other hand, when somebody tells us a good story, we tend to accept and embrace it.

Stories differ from other forms of communication because people don't resist them. Story is non-invasive and nonthreatening. We believe stories more than rational argument or other types of discourse. The more a company like mydeco.com provides stories that truly help us decorate, the more likely we are to see them as people we can trust, and people we can purchase from with confidence.

What does all this mean about corporate communication in general? In the section of this chapter where I discuss treating community management as "a process of relationship building", I advocate not trying to sell people something straight away, but rather thinking about how to engage them in a relationship that builds trust. In our email messages, on our websites, and on our social media pages, we should seek first and foremost to win and maintain the trust of our clients and prospects. One of the best ways to do this is by telling compelling – and authentic – stories.

"

"If it is a good story, you don't have to keep it alive by yourself. It is automatically retold or replayed in the minds of your listeners."

Annette Simmons, *The Story Factor*

"

ENCOURAGE USER-GENERATED CONTENT

As I discussed in chapters 2 and 4, companies today seem to be discovering and beginning to use storytelling in their communication with their followers. In particular, marketers are discovering the power of user-generated stories.

User stories have even more credibility than company-generated stories. In the previous section, we saw the importance of providing our stories to our communities. At the same time, recipients of <u>corporate</u> messages tend to be distrustful, and thus companies should seek out <u>users</u> with interesting stories, and encourage them to share their tales with the community.

For example, when a design company such as mydeco. com states that they will inspire us with interior design ideas, we may not believe it completely at first, since it is a company talking to us. When clients tell <u>their</u> stories of how <u>they</u> were inspired by mydeco.com, it is far more credible, because "people like us" are doing the talking.

In today's world, where we co-create brands with the brand community, these user-generated stories often shape brand identity more than the company's own marketing messages.

So, along with providing your stories to the community, think about innovative ways to get users to bring <u>their</u>

stories to the community. In so doing, we should **seek out existing stories**, and also use our email lists and social media pages to **generate new ones**.

Some companies are becoming skillful at uncovering the "stories out there". In fact, in my discussions with companies about how they generate user stories, I am surprised by the number of people who tell me that the stories already exist on the web. When companies such as Filofax or mydeco.com monitor the Internet "buzz" around their brands, they find people talking about them in blogs and on the social networks. It turns out that passionate user communities exist in many places today, and not only for trendy or glamorous merchandise. People simply love to tell the stories of how they use products, and they do it perhaps more than we realize.

How do you get users to contribute their stories? Human beings love to tell stories; usually, all we have to do is get them started. As we saw in an earlier section of this chapter, one easy way to begin is with your **email list**. Send a mailing asking people to write a story about something related to your product. For example, in early 2010, the famous French ski town Val d'Isère sent an email asking followers for stories of their first visit to the town. To encourage participation, they gave away some small prizes.

Generating user content is an arena where email, social and storytelling can all work together. First, send out an email to announce the "tell your story of...whatever" contest. Then, publicize the contest across all your channels – blog, website, Facebook page, Twitter, etc. – and encourage your fans to spread the word to others. When you begin to collect interesting stories, take some of the best ones and turn the writers into "stars" by publishing their tales in your email newsletter. Turning fans into stars is good for brand awareness; the stars will almost certainly want to show off their "exploits" by forwarding your newsletter to their friends.

One of the keys to generating user content is looking for creative ways to trigger stories in the mind of the listener. For instance, if you write a blog about an experience that is widely shared by members of the community, they will often respond with their own versions around similar themes. When Filofax shares tales of "my first Filofax" or "the time I thought I lost my Filofax", others automatically think of similar stories that they could contribute.

Your followers will be more likely to contribute their stories, ideas or photos if you manage to discover and leverage passion points. One way to tap into user passion is to **run contests and issue challenges.** For example, mydeco.com shows their "top 5 room designs" on their website, with the following challenge: Think you could do better? Pit yourself against the professionals and show us what you can do with our fabulous 3D room planner tools.

Any company can generate them. People are often passionate about their daily activities and the products associated with them. In fact, there is nothing inherently "sexy" about the way we organize our personal information (Filofax), prepare our meals (Mathon), or decorate our homes (mydeco.com). But, we may feel strongly about the ways we do these things, and we are quite willing to share our thoughts with others.

One of the questions I am asked most often after my presentations at industry conferences involves what to do if a product or service is not particularly glamorous, hot or trendy: "We don't really have stories to tell because our product, or service, is just not sexy. Our clients don't really have stories either. How can we generate user content?"

No matter what your business activity, you can talk about something you do well, emphasize it, and collect user stories about it. If you have great customer service, or service recovery, customers will be more than happy to tell the world about their experiences. Some outstanding retail companies, such as Nordstrom, Marks & Spencer or LL Bean, have built enduring reputations around their customer service, and their client stories have become legend.

You can look for innovative ways to tap into user **passion about a related activity**. Mathon may sell pots and pans, but they have learned to generate significant quantities of user content and comments, not so much around their product itself but around the activity of cooking. Their Facebook page is often humming with activity, because people are enthusiastic about comparing recipes, showing photos of their creations, and telling of childhood memories related to one of the recipes posted by the company or by another user.

With their community of fans and a bit of imagination, Mathon has created a virtual tribe. One can imagine that, hundreds of years ago, people sat around campfires telling stories of their recipes. Now they can do the same thing online without even knowing each other.

66

"One of the most effective things we ever did was to start giving match tickets and team jerseys to our most influential bloggers. We help them by providing these prizes to make their blogs more attractive and entertaining, and they help us by serving as our 'eyes and ears' in the fan community. Today, many of them feel like partners to us, and they have a true sense of belonging to a 'PSG family'. They have become some of our best advocates."

Julien Jalouzet, community manager, Paris Saint-Germain football club

99

PROMOTE YOUR PROMOTERS

Find your potential advocates and ambassadors. Where do you find the people who are promoting you, or those who might if given the opportunity? One logical place to begin is your own email list. As we saw in the case of Mathon, simply sending an email asking clients and prospects to visit their Facebook page yielded impressive results. In less than 48 hours, more than 10,000 people had "liked" the page. In addition, numerous recipients wrote back to thank the company for the invitation. Many of these fans have evolved into regular visitors to the page, and some are even active advocates for the company.

Another place to look for supporters is among your followers on Twitter. When Domino's Pizza updated their pizza recipe in their well-documented Pizza Turnaround Campaign, they asked customers to leave comments via the hashtag #newpizza. Not only did they engage many of their fans in the process, they were also able to track contact with many of their most active followers.

You can also explore what consumers are saying about your brand by watching blogs and social sites, either on your own or using "buzz monitoring" services and software. Watching this sort of activity allows you to identify the people most interested in what you are doing. As such, mydeco.com keeps a "massive list" of bloggers relative to their company and also to design in general. Julien Jalouzet, community manager at the Paris Saint-Germain football club, says that fans of the team are extremely active on social networks. So, he follows activity on Facebook, particularly on the many group pages about the PSG or its individual players.

Make them part of your journey. The customers and fans who actively promote you deserve special treatment, and the best way to make them feel special is to make them feel like insiders. In fact, I often tell the companies I work with that their goal should be to build a culture where all the key stakeholders feel like insiders, and this would certainly include your best customers.

Making customers feel part of your culture and your journey can be accomplished in small and simple ways. For example, Dunkin' Donuts chooses each week a different fan photo to be its official Facebook profile picture. Of course, the chosen fan wants all of his friends to see him in action, and this drives traffic to Dunkin's Facebook page and website.

Some companies are starting to realize the influence of bloggers, and they have begun using them to promote their brands. As the opening quote for this section indicates, Paris Saint-Germain football club tries to build relationships with influential blogs by offering them team jerseys, match tickets, and exclusive content. The bloggers, in turn, provide information to the team, for example suggestions about what people would like to see in email newsletters or on the PSG Facebook page. Community manager Julien Jalouzet says that the support of bloggers has truly helped the marketing group communicate more effectively with the fan base.

Similarly, mydeco.com reaches out to their "top 50" bloggers every month with content chosen for them, including the most interesting ideas or videos that the company has identified since their last contact. And, to give these promoters a sense of belonging to an inner circle, they sponsor periodic blogger meet-ups for exchange of ideas.

Co-create with them. It is not only bloggers who can become "brand insiders". Coca-Cola has the most active brand-related page on Facebook, according to the *Financial Times*, with more than 3 million members. What many Coke fans may not realize is that the page was actually started by two enthusiasts, an actor and a writer, who did it for fun, invited a few of their friends, and watched the phenomenon grow.

Today, the page is jointly administered by Coca-Cola and the page's founders, and it has become an enormous asset for the company. Most of the content is simply from fans sharing stories about how Coke is part of their lives. According to Coca-Cola's group director of worldwide interactive marketing, Michael Donnelly, the page is "a great way for us to expose a huge number of people to what we're doing at no cost."

The page's founding duo is not paid for their work on the page, but they are treated as important people, and the company co-creates content with them. For example, in January 2009, Coca-Cola flew them to its headquarters in Atlanta, where they made a fanciful video about the experience and posted it to the Facebook page. The fans loved it!

Another example of partnership between brand and consumer is the PSG Facebook page. The marketing group often chooses fans and allows them to write their observations on the official team page. According to the PSG's community manager, this co-creation initiative has generated increased interest in the page, probably because the "chosen" fan tells all his friends and contacts about his contribution. These friends, in turn, click the "Like" button and become fans of PSG's page as well.

Turn your fans into advocates by involving them in product creation. What is the effect when Domino's Pizza asks customers to tweet their impressions and criticism of the latest recipe, or when Dunkin' Donuts runs their annual online "create the next donut" contest? Those who participate become advocates! Since they want to tell their "tribe" what they have been up to, they tweet it or post it on social media pages in their status updates. Each time people choose to share in these ways creates a chance for the company to garner new fans. And, since Dunkin's "next donut" contest drew nearly 300,000 entries in 2010, the online word-of-mouth effect was striking.

Create interesting little moments that let your fans engage, and they will repay you with free or low-cost

advertising. When Dunkin' Donuts offered an Internet discount coupon to all customers who submitted photos of themselves drinking iced coffee in winter, the results were impressive. One hundred forty entries generated nearly 4 million product plugs through posts and status updates on the social sites. Such online initiatives help spread a positive image of the company. In fact, Vivaldi Partners reported in 2010 that people were 50% more likely to have heard good things about Dunkin' Donuts than about its competitor Starbucks.

CHAPTER 6
The case
of Filofax

This chapter consists of excerpts from several interviews with Jessica Stephens. The interviews took place during 2010, when Jessica served as group marketing manager at Filofax. The purpose of this chapter is to show one extended example of a company that is quietly implementing many of the concepts of this book to manage an active brand community. Filofax not only uses email, social media and storytelling effectively, they find synergies between the three activities.

The first time we talked, you told me you use storytelling extensively. Could you tell me more about that?

I think Filofax is very lucky in that our product naturally lends itself to storytelling. Our tagline is "Filofax. It's a way of life", which sums up the idea of my Filofax being more than just a bunch of dates: It's everything I do and it's everything about me. As a result, our customers' stories are very personal and evoke a highly emotional response. For us this is the next stage in customer attention and loyalty; if you can get people to truly engage with your brand on an emotional level, they are likely to become lifelong customers. This emotional relationship with our customers gives our brand a competitive advantage.

We're very privileged to be in this position. We leverage it in almost all of our channels: We tell the customers' stories through email and use social networks to the same effect, with very good response. People are very willing to tell their stories and, moreover, people want to hear other people's stories.

How do you generate customer stories?

Sometimes stories happen organically. Followers of our blog, Facebook, Twitter and Flickr pages talk amongst themselves, and some of the stories that emanate from there come to have a life of their own.

One thing we discovered was that there are a lot of stories out there, and that we could uncover them with an email message or with a question on Facebook. For example, if we ask for comments by email about a specific theme such as "tell us about a time when you lost your Filofax and how you felt", we can collect lots of user stories, and some surprisingly emotional ones.

But it makes sense, really, all the emotion. If you imagine peoples' whole lives are in there – phone numbers, appointments, addresses, personal notes – it is easy to understand their fear of losing their Filofax. A lot of the stories were indeed of people who lost their Filofax on a train, a plane or just somewhere, and actually had it returned to them. In their stories they talk about this fantastic sense of relief when they received their Filofax back. They felt like they had their life back in their hands.

We can also instigate stories on Facebook. When we asked for instance, "How did you get your first Filofax?" the responses we got were really quite fascinating. The emotional attachment people have to their Filofax is massive. So, they write very personal stories. One girl told us about how she went out with her mother specifically to buy a personal organizer. The words she used were really interesting, because she opened the organizer up and she saw the stamp inside of the leather saying "made in England, real calf leather". She said: "that stamp changed my life". Those were her exact words, "it changed my life". That's the kind of thing we find and that's the kind of people we have the honor of working with. It's our customers who define this product as "life changing" for them.

We always try to think of new and interesting questions to ask our fans. But the fascinating thing is, whatever the question, there are always stories. We only have to ask a hint of a question and we get all of this response back.

How do you choose which social spaces to be in?

Rather than just looking at which social spaces are popular, we select those spaces that are appropriate to us and that are used by our target market, mainly consisting of students and professionals.

We have a very high level of engagement on Facebook, with the stories of course, but also with people's comments and ideas about the products. Twitter is great for the instant feedback on a new idea, and also to find out if there's a trendy topic that's relevant to us.

I should also mention the important role of Flickr for us. A lot of our designs are aimed at the female fashion market, and Flickr is a great place to showcase a product that people might visualize.

How do you use email?

Of course, one of our uses of email is just a fairly traditional newsletter format. There, we do have the advantage of a highly engaged customer email database. Email has also been great as a sales channel for us, and it is still our best way of getting information to clients. We use quite a lot of trigger emails and targeting. We like to send customized messages to notify people of specific products, at the specific times when they are most likely to want them.

As I said before, we also use email to generate user stories about how people use their Filofax, what it feels like to lose it, etc. And then, we use the newsletter to share the most interesting or remarkable stories from the community. In this arena, I think we can use email even more extensively than we have been doing. We find that email newsletters are great for spreading user stories, and that people love to share this way.

Do you have an in-house email system, or do you outsource?

We use Emailvision. They have developed vast expertise in today's issues of e-marketing: deliverability, tracking results, personalizing messages, and integrating email with social media. Emailvision has the specialized people and resources to help us do these things better than we could do them in-house.

So, we like having a specialized professional service company to support us in managing our email delivery and tracking, but also to help us cross-fertilize our email and social media activities. In addition, since we are a global company, having a service provider with truly local presence in the various countries gives us the possibility to adapt our use of email to the specific markets. One could make the choice to do all of these activities in-house. But for us it made sense to do this in collaboration with a dedicated and focused company.

How would you describe the overall goals of your engagement in social media and email?

Well, first of all, you want to be where the customer is. And our customers are out there in the social space sharing their stories and experiences with each other. For a brand it is great to be involved in this movement. When we listen, we find out what's important to our clients and how we can better serve them with our products.

But also, nowadays you simply have to be in the social space because your customers expect you to be there. We actually got involved in the social space because people made us aware of the conversations about us that were taking place on the web.

We also see the social networks as sort of customer incubators. Someone might not be a customer right now, but you know there's an interest there and at some point you hope to be able to convert them. So we're sort of playing the long game with these groups. That is where email comes in as well. We have a "sign up for our email newsletter" on our Facebook pages, and we've got some good response from that.

Email is great for maintaining regular contact, and also for personalizing the contact with individuals. We definitely want to develop this personalization further in the future. There are some interesting technical developments happening in email services that make it more possible to send more "custom tailored" email campaigns.

You said that you got involved in social media because you were made aware of the conversations that were taking place on the web about you. Could you talk more about that?

Actually it was the people behind the blog 'Philofaxy' that inspired us to step into the social media space and made us realize that conversations were happening that we should be involved in. Philofaxy's tagline is 'for the love of Filofax'. It's simply for people who love their Filofax. These are our most incredible brand advocates. They are collectors, and typically they will have between 6 and 10 personal Filofax organizers within their own collection. They are very active within the social space.

They have a blog but they also have a Facebook page and a Twitter page and I'm happy to say that we have a fantastic relationship with them online, which for example means that we will retweet their tweets, and they will retweet us.

We follow the hashtag 'Philofaxy', and we can see that they engage with our content so much. Also they are super users of our product, and as individuals they are super users of the social networks. This means their reach is huge. So the Filofax message is spread far and wide by these people who absolutely adore the product. I mean, you can't pay for that kind of thing.

How do you create multiple touch points between channels?

Rather than viewing a channel specifically as being able to do one thing, we have integrated marketing campaigns. For example, considering all the valuable content that's being produced on the social networks, it makes natural sense to incorporate that into our newsletter and email campaigns.

When we share user content from the social sites, for example telling customer stories in our email newsletter or in a separate campaign...that can be very effective. Those types of stories are often some of the most popular content we send.

I suppose, like most companies, we've added "follow us on Facebook or Twitter" at the bottom of our emails. But something we're considering doing in the coming weeks is to issue an exclusive Facebook invitation. In other words, sending out an email campaign to ask people to become fans of our Facebook page...simply because we know people are interested in the stories that have been generated by our users on the networks. So why not become a fan and have that information in your newsfeed on a daily basis?

Many times it's not the company promotion that draws people in, it's the human relationships and the emotional stories that make people want to go and join that group. So that's a real plus point for Filofax because we naturally have those stories and those enthusiastic users.

How do you create synergy between social media, email and storytelling?

We use stories from the social networks in our email messages to clients and prospects, stories about Filofaxes that were gifts from loved ones, or about how people got them for a first job, or examples of how they have upgraded them. These shared stories not only form the basis of the Filofax community, they put on display all the enthusiasm around the product. This enables us to connect to potential customers on an emotional level.

In one of our conferences you talked about "leveraging the passion point". What do you mean by that?

The Filofax e-marketing strategy, using both social and email, is all based around this notion of leveraging the passion point. The passion points for Filofax are people's need and desire to organize themselves, and their love for the Filofax product itself. People who are organized in their daily lives accomplish more, see more people and do more interesting things. As for the product itself, people really go for the leather bound personal organizer.

All this works very well in the social space. Instead of asking people to just "like" our service, we ask them to talk about their lives and passions. Exploring the passion point leads to very interesting results in terms of the stories and testimonials we generate.

How do you evaluate the impact of your efforts with email and social media?

We've recently done a data audit and discovered that, at least among people on our email list, our customers really want to hear what we are saying. They tell us that they want more stories from us. We also know from our experience integrating email and social that the two channels are closely connected. For example, we always notice higher levels of engagement on our social networks after we've included a good story in an email newsletter.

One thing that is very important to us is that we don't want to chase numbers. In other words, we are not looking to have millions of fans if those fans are not truly interested in what's happening on the site. Instead, we track engagement levels: the average length of stay for visitors to the site, or the number and types of comments generated by a post. These are not exact measures, but they help us estimate the number of truly engaged people.

If you watch the number of comments per post over time, and plot it against the total number of users who are following you, you can come up with an engagement metric, one that can give you insight about how active your fans are. At Filofax, it's really important for us to keep that engagement metric at the same level or growing, no matter how many subscribers we have. Again, I emphasize that we're not interested in getting millions of people to join us if they are not really engaged with the product, and if they don't want to hear and share the stories. People who become fans but are not active are less likely to become customers later.

Anyway, none of this is an exact science, but it is interesting to watch. As I say, one thing we do try to get a handle on every month is the engagement metric. Over time, I think we and others will find more sophisticated ways of gauging these levels of user activity and involvement. It is all heading in that direction: more and better measurement and understanding of user behavior.

How do you use different channels to communicate with your clients?

As a rule, we try to keep all communication on the page from which it originated. So if someone contacts us on Twitter, we retweet. We send a direct personal message if something is sensitive in nature, but generally we try to keep the activity on the network. If the follower or customer requests to have that email contact one to one, then we will provide the resource for that relationship.

So basically it's whatever the customer says, goes, because we believe that we need to be where the customer is. In addition, we think that part of our service involves communicating in the way the customer wants to communicate. We like to fit in with the conversation rather than trying to direct or dominate it.

You talk about maintaining a conversation with your target audience. How frequently do you want to be in touch with them?

An interesting question about email marketing has always been around frequency. Companies have been very anxious about appearing too frequently, or not frequently enough, in an individual's inbox. These are questions we deal with daily in our email program. How do we find the right balance?

Today, you have totally new inboxes, like your fans' Facebook inboxes, where you can send updates directly to the fans, and that opens a whole load of new questions. Should we use Facebook email in addition to traditional email? What will people come to use and expect us to use? How often should we use that medium?

What we tend to do at Filofax is stick to the same rule that we use in our email marketing. Unless we have something very interesting to say in a particular place, we will not use that channel. We wouldn't just appear in their Facebook inbox for the hell of it, because that tends to be a very personal space. We also don't want to be over-communicating, since people can find that annoying. We feel it should not be about the frequency of our messages but rather about learning to talk effectively when we have something significant to say.

How do you "listen" to your community?

We listen in three ways. The first way is that people want to communicate product suggestions to us; some of these ideas we actually pass on to our product development team. We've had so many product comments on Facebook that we now create a monthly document that goes to our product development team to advise them on what the customers want and what they are actually saying about our product. Of course, some of these ideas we've had before, but others are completely new and very exciting.

The second way we listen is simply monitoring online chat of the sort, "I love my iPhone or Blackberry and

I would never stop using it, but I cannot give up my Filofax". We like to invite these people to join our community, because they tend to become active in the discussions, and they tend to write nice things on our wall for others to see.

The third way is monitoring more general topics. Twitter is great for instant feedback, and also for finding out about trendy themes in areas that are relevant to us. For example, we like to hear interesting ideas about how people organize their lives and their work, and it's sometimes nice for us to be able to join those conversations. So, we follow certain keywords and see if it might be appropriate to participate in a discussion. When we do jump in, people often initially think: "Filofax? What are they doing here?" and then usually change their mind and appreciate us being there. Our idea is to be quietly engaged and present in spaces where we are not necessarily expected.

There are also a small number of highly engaged people, who not only love our product, but are constantly blogging, tweeting, and are always out there in the space. We like to form individual relationships with these influencers. We get in touch with them by sending them a direct message, using social media, and we then often maintain regular email contact with them. These people tend to really appreciate the personal email exchanges with us. We also organize blogger events, just to understand what is happening in that space.

I have heard you use the expression of "taking control by letting go". What exactly do you mean by that, and how does it work?

It's more important to try to understand and listen to a community than to try and control it. If you try to control a social community, you are definitely going to run into issues.

There's probably a lot of fear in most companies around the notion of letting go. This is a completely new direction for most brands. Today, the world is moving away from push media that says: "This is my brand, this is how we want to appear", to "How do you in the community perceive us?" All this can be dangerous unless you have a really good product and you provide excellent service. I think that as long as you've got those two boxes ticked, you actually <u>should</u> give up control, because you've got nothing to hide. I think that the casualties of the new social media revolution are going to be those people who potentially don't have the best product or service, because bad news is going to get out there in a much greater way than it ever has before.

Last year we actually launched an online product in the UK to bloggers before launching it to the traditional press. The bloggers were grateful that we took the time to acknowledge them before the traditional press. But what happened was, unlike the brand guidelines that you can distribute to the press, the bloggers will not be told what to write about your brand. This led to a proliferation of content that was sometimes not exactly what we would have wanted to say about our brand, but it was still all very positive. The only way for us to take control was by letting go and giving the brand over to these bloggers, which led in the end to a fantastic result and to a closer relationship with the bloggers.

When you let go of control, how do you deal with the negative comments that every company at some point faces?

We don't have many negative things coming up. The most negative thing that we pick up on our monitoring is: "Why would you use a Filofax? Why wouldn't you be modern and just use an electronic organizer?" And it's interesting that a great deal of our demographic use both. So when somebody writes something critical like "why should anyone these days still use a Filofax?", you get responses from the community about all the advantages of a Filofax in today's world. It feels so great when the community responds to defend your brand!

Many people think of Filofax as a tech-averse product, but we don't fear technology in any way. In fact, we embrace it. There are even plans to move into that sector in the future. But for now, and we think for a long time to come, people enjoy something tangible. They simply like to write things down. And in fact, I would go so far as to say that people will probably never stop writing things down.

How do you see the future of social networks for Filofax?

I can definitely see marketplace activity and even direct selling happening on social networks, even though this will probably never be a substitute for our original homepage, which continues to be our number one site for e-commerce. If you're someone who's already a Filofax customer and you quickly want your refill, you may want to order it through Facebook because you already have that relationship with us. But I don't think we will set up shops on social networks. We think of our Facebook pages like satellite home pages. At the moment we have one international Facebook page, but I think at some point it will make sense to have separate pages for each specific market and language.

END NOTES

Information on the following companies comes from personal interviews

Paris Saint-Germain – Julien Jalouzet

Mathon (from video interview by Sébastien Levaillant)

U-Switch – Simon Hills

Filofax – Jessica Stephens

mydeco.com – Joanne Casley

Quotes from these industry experts also are from personal conversations

Nick Heys – founder and CEO, Emailvision

Hans Christian Wilson – founder, High and Low adventure park

Johann Füller – founder, Hyve AG; Assistant Professor, University of Innsbruck; Research Affiliate, Sloan School of Management MIT

Chapter 1

Reference to the book the *Seven Rules of Storytelling*:

SADOWSKY, J. & ROCHE, L. (2009) : *Les sept règles du storytelling*, Editions Pearson France

Linked-In plan for Company Pages

http://www.mycustomer.com/topic/marketing/how-will-linkedinscompany-pages-impact-social-media-marketing/116275

Chapter 2

Quotes

WIESEL, E. (1966) *The Gates to the Forest*, New York, Holt, Rinehart & Winston.

TURNER, M. (1996) *The literary mind*, New York, Oxford University Press.

BLIXEN, K. (1986) *The Last Tales*, London, Penguin Books.

BARTHES, R. (1966) *Introduction to the Structural Analysis of Narratives*, in HEATH, S. (Ed.) Image – Music – Text. Glasgow, Collins.

LE GUIN, U. K. (1989) *Dancing at the edge of the world: thoughts on words, women, places*, New York, Grove Press.

SARTRE, J.-P. (1965) *Nausea*, London, Penguin.

SHEEHY, G. (1995) *New Passages: Mapping Your Life Across Time*, New York, Random House.

SIMMONS, A. (2001) *The story factor: secrets of influence from the art of storytelling,* Cambridge, Mass., Perseus Pub.

MACINTYRE, A. C. (1984) *After virtue: a study in moral theory,* Notre Dame, Ind., University of Notre Dame Press.

BRUNER, J. S. (1986) *Actual minds, possible worlds,* Cambridge, Mass., Harvard University Press.

BETTELHEIM, B. (1976) *The uses of enchantment: the meaning and importance of fairy tales*, New York, Knopf: distributed by Random House.

SCHANK, R. C. (1995) *Tell me a story: narrative and intelligence,* Evanston, Ill., Northwestern University Press.

CARD, O. S. (1990) *Maps in a mirror: the short fiction of Orson Scott Card*, New York, Tor Books.

TICHY, N. M. & COHEN, E. B. (1997) *The leadership engine: how winning companies build leaders at every level*, New York, Harper Business.

PINK, D. H. (2006) *A whole new mind: why right brainers will rule the future*, New York, Riverhead Books.

KEEN, S. & FOX, A. V. (1989) *Your mythic journey: finding meaning in your life through writing and storytelling*, Los Angeles, J.P. Tarcher.

FULFORD, R. (2000) *The triumph of narrative: storytelling in the age of mass culture*, New York, Broadway Books.

KING, L. (2006) "Film about suicide opens in theatres" *Larry King Live*. Los Angeles, CNN.

KEEN, S. & FOX, A. V. (1989) *Your mythic journey: finding meaning in your life through writing and storytelling*, Los Angeles, J.P. Tarcher.

NEUHAUSER, P. (1993) *Corporate legends and lore: the power of storytelling as a management tool*, New York, McGraw-Hill.

DENNING, S. (2001) *The springboard : how storytelling ignites action in knowledge-era organizations*, Boston, Butterworth-Heinemann.

Other sources on narrative

CZARNIAWSKA-JOERGES, B. (1998) *Narrative approach to organization studies*, Thousand Oaks, CA, Sage Publications.

POLKINGHORNE, D. (1988) *Narrative knowing and the human sciences,* Albany, State University of New York Press.

WEICK, K. E. (1995) *Sensemaking in organizations*, Thousand Oaks, Sage Publications.

Old Spice

http://www.niemanlab.org/2010/07/no-seriously-what-the-oldspice-ads-can-teach-us-about-news-future/?=sidelink;

http://www.niemanlab.org/2009/07/how-viral-culture-is-changinghow-we-learn-share-create-and-interact

Chapter 3

Quotes

BEDBURY, SCOTT:

http://www.fastcompany.com/online/10/bedbury.
html

EINSTEIN, A. (2006) Einstein Quotes

http://zaadz.com/quotes/topics/simplicity

WHYTE, D. (2001) *Crossing the unknown sea: work as a pilgrimage of identity*, New York, Riverhead Books.

TWAIN, MARK:

http://www.submityourarticle.com/articles/Steve-Shaw-1/articlemarketing-79306.php

Timberland

BIRCHALL, J. "The outdoor boss trying to tread an ethical path", *Financial Times*, 10 October 2010, p. 16

Margaret Thatcher

LITTLE, G. (1988) Strong leadership : *Thatcher, Reagan and an Eminent Person*, Melbourne ; New York, Oxford University Press. GARDNER, H. & LASKIN, E. (1995) *Leading minds: an anatomy of leadership*, New York, NY, BasicBooks.

Paul Dolan and Fetzer Vineyards

DOLAN, P. (2003) *True to our roots: fermenting a business revolution*, Princeton, N.J., Bloomberg Press.

Bike Friday

www.bikefriday.com

Phil Jackson

JACKSON, P. & DELEHANTY, H. (1995) *Sacred Hoops: Spiritual Lessons of a Hardwood Warrior*, New York, Hyperion.

Steve Jobs and the Macintosh team

BENNIS, W. G. & BIEDERMAN, P. W. (1997) *Organizing genius: the secrets of creative collaboration*, Reading, Mass., Addison- Wesley.

Chapter 4

P&G Pampers incident

http://www.ft.com/cms/s/0/5622eb4e-6926-11df-aa7e-00144feab49a.html

http://www.csmonitor.com/Business/2010/0510/
Facebook-parentspush-for-Pampers-recall

http://blog.hubspot.com/blog/tabid/6307/
bid/5518/Why-Pampers-Diaper-Fail-is-a-Lesson-in-
Marketing-Transparency.aspx

http://www.mikevolpe.com/bid/12713/Thoughts-
on-the-Pampers-Social-Media-Marketing-Disaster

http://adage.com/article?article_id=143963

Facebook growth

http://www.ft.com/cms/s/0/8410ad22-9511-11df-
b2e1-00144feab49a.html

Fibertel in Argentina

http://www.clarin.com/politica/gobierno/Masiva-
reaccion-intentocierre-Fibertel_0_320967950.html

http://www.clarin.com/politica/defensor-Pueblo-
investigacionintento-Fibertel_0_323367838.html

Eurostar

http://www.brandrepublic.com/News/974801/
Crisis-hit-Eurostardiscovers-social-media-users-want-
marketing/

http://eu.techcrunch.com/2009/12/19/as-hundreds-of-eurostarpassengers-languish-eurostar-ignores-twitter

Adidas versus Nike

"Football battle between Nike and Adidas intensifies off pitch", *Financial Times,* June 11, 2010 p. 17

"Adidas pulls ahead of Nike in online World Cup marketing battle", *The Guardian,* 11 June 2010

Chapter 5

Quotes

DODSON, FITZHUGH:

http://www.worldofquotes.com/author/Fitzhugh-Dodson/1/index.html 5

RUMI: http://www.squidoo.com/rumi-quotes

CHAMP, HEATHER: http://5by5.tv/pipeline/21

BEDBURY, SCOTT:

http://www.fastcompany.com/online/10/bedbury.html

SIMMONS, A. (2001) *The story factor: secrets of influence from the art of storytelling*, Cambridge, Mass., Perseus Pub

United Airlines

http://www.time.com/time/specials/packages/article/0,28804,1945379_1945171_1945170,00.html

http://www.squidoo.com/united-breaks-guitars

Nestlé

http://www.independent.co.uk/environment/green-living/onlineprotest-drives-nestl-to-environmentally-friendly-palm-oil-1976443.html

http://news.mongabay.com/2010/0517-hance_nestle.html

Obama's use of social media

http://www.fastcompany.com/1698848/barack-obamas-postelection-social-media-lapse?#

Coca-Cola and Facebook

http://www.ft.com/cms/s/0/3b8b4cf2-230b-11de-9c99-00144feabdc0.html

Dunkin Donuts, Starbucks, and social currency

http://www.fastcompany.com/magazine/145/next-tech-five-stepsto-social-currency.html

(The Vivaldi Partners study on social currency can be accessed through the *Fast Company* article)

Defining social currency

http://theforestandthetrees.com/the_forest_%26_the_trees/the_forest_—26_the_trees_-_Social_Currency_Marketing_-_Connect._Converse._Partner._Grow..html

Domino's Pizza

http://www.pizzaturnaround.com

Made in the USA
San Bernardino, CA
15 July 2014